SUMPTUOUS PATCHWORK

Edited by
CHRISTINE DONALDSON

30 Exciting and Original Patchwork Projects
Embellished with embroidery, beading & stencilling

Original Projects by:

Christine Donaldson
Gisela Thwaites

Jill Essery
Gilly Wraight

Trafalgar Square Publishing

ACKNOWLEDGEMENTS

*Savitri Books would like to give their sincere thanks
to Anne and Roddy Dewe, who allowed their house to be used
as a 'location' and offered many artifacts and kindnesses.
To Emma Andrew, whose elegance and charm brought
some of the projects to life. To Sarah Dewe,
our photographer, whose contribution cannot be overrated,
and last, but not least, to the four ladies whose hard work
and creativity made this book possible.*

❦

First published in the United States of America in 1997 by
Trafalgar Square Publishing, North Pomfret, Vermont 05053

Printed and bound in Spain

© Savitri Books (this edition, all photographs and design), 1997
© Christine Donaldson (text and projects), 1997
© Gisela Thwaites (text and projects), 1997
© Jill Essery (text and projects), 1997
© Gilly Wraight (text and projects), 1997

Library of Congress Catalog Card Number: 96-60657

ISBN: 1-57076-068-3

Conceived, produced and designed by
SAVITRI BOOKS LTD
115J Cleveland Street
London W1P 5PN

Art direction and design by Mrinalini Srivastava
Photography by Sarah Dewe
Edited by Caroline Taggart

Typeset in Melior by Type Technique, London, United Kingdom
Reproduced by Regent Publishing Services, Hong Kong
Printed and bound by Gráficas Reunidas, Spain

NOTE ON COPYRIGHT

CONTENTS

❧

HOW TO USE THIS BOOK

Sumptuous Patchwork contains 30 original projects. Some have been grouped and can be produced singly or as a complete set. The four makers who devised these exciting designs rank among the foremost exponents of embellished patchwork, creating stunning effects by combining patchwork and applique with hand and machine embroidery, beading, cording, stencilling and many other attractive techniques.

Before embarking on a project, it is advisable to read the *entire* text first and to work in the suggested sequence. In most cases, the templates and patterns have been reproduced quarter or half size, depending on the dimensions of the original. In the case of the garment patterns, the design also includes a grid to enable you to transfer the pattern to squared-up paper, if you prefer. Otherwise, use a photocopier to do the necessary enlargements. In some cases, you will need to do this in sections and join the pieces to obtain the entire pattern. Always check the percentages carefully.

All the techniques used in the book have been fully explained, most of them with step-by-step photographs. You will also probably wish to use *Sumptuous Patchwork* as a source book to create your own designs and to inspire you to develop your personal style of embellishments.

THE QUILTERS

Christine Donaldson is a quilt-maker and embroiderer who studied design and embroidery at Loughborough College of Art and Design. She exhibits regularly with the Milton Keynes Craft Guild. Much of her work involves commissions for ecclesiastical embroidery. Her first book, *Patchwork Baby*, was published in 1994. She works to commission. She can be contacted at: *75 Overn Avenue, Buckingham MK18 1LU, United Kingdom.*

Gisela Thwaites is a prestigious quilt-maker with a passionate interest in Indian embroidery and quilting techniques. German born, she pioneered the techniques of embellished patchwork in this country, where she is equally well known for her more traditional work. She has been a judge at The National Patchwork Championship and at The Great British Quilt Festival. Her quilts sell at Liberty or are made to commission. She can be contacted at: *Rose Cottage, Rusper Road, Newdigate, Dorking, Surrey RH5 5BX, United Kingdom.*

Jill Essery was born in Australia but she has lived for over twenty years in England where she studied patchwork, applique and embroidery for the City and Guilds Diploma. She pieces, quilts and embroiders beautiful jackets and weaistcoats, richly textured wall hangings and textile jewellery. She is a member of the Suffolk Craft Society with whom she exhibits regularly. She works to commission. She can be contacted at: *Blackberry Barn, Mill Street, Gislingham, Eye, Suffolk IP23 8JR, United Kingdom.*

Gilly Wraight is a freelance textile artist, embroiderer and lecturer. She studied patchwork and embroidery for her City and Guilds Diploma. Since 1996 she has been an Associate of the Embroiderers' Development Scheme of the Embroiderers' Guild. She can be contacted at: *Stable House, Winkfield Road, Ascot, Berkshire SL5 7LT, United Kingdom.*

'NOSTALGIA' APPLIQUED PICTURE & STENCILLED FRAME

❧

Christine Donaldson

A careful choice of old-fashioned printed fabrics and 'found' objects, such as old buttons, make this picture in its stencilled and quilted frame look as if it was made a long time ago. The scraps of fabric can be dipped in tea if they look too new. The frame can also be made on its own to enclose an old photograph or a mirror.

1. Out of the unbleached calico, cut 1 oblong 9 x 7 in / 23 x 18 cm. Use the blunt end of a pencil or a piece of dowel with a diameter of approximately ¼ in / 6 mm to 'print' small circles, using gold paint. Distribute these over the surface of the calico, as you wish. Dry and fix, according to the manufacturer's instructions.

2. Enlarge the pattern on page 12 as instructed. Make paper templates of the numbered applique pieces in the central motif and transfer on to freezer paper (see paragraphs 3. and 4. of pages 75-76). Applique all of the shapes in order, except for tulip No. 4., which encroaches over the border.

3. **The inner border.** Cut 1½ in / 38 mm wide strips out of the printed cotton fabrics to form a border to the central panel in the order marked: a. – d. In order to get the authentic scrap-quilt effect, join 2 fabrics in at least 1 of the strips. The border can be stitched on the machine, but the seams have a softer appearance if you work them by hand with a running stitch – and it doesn't take much longer than on the machine! Press seams outwards and applique the remaining flower shape. Make tiny slits at the back of each appliqued shape and pull out the freezer paper template.

4. **The blue outer border.** Measure 1 short side of the picture and cut 2 strips of the blue striped cotton to that length and 4 in / 10 cm wide. Join them on to the picture. Measure 1 long side, cut 2 strips to that length and the same width as before and join them to the picture.

5. **The curvilinear pattern.** Cut out the outline on the paper pattern prepared in 2. above and use this 'template' to trace a guide line for the curvilinear 'stems' on the blue border. Cut a bias strip, 1¼ in / 32 mm wide. Join if necessary to make 50 in / 1.27 m. Fold in half lengthwise, with right sides together, and machine-stitch ¼ in / 6 mm from the edge to form a tube. Trim the seam, then turn right side out, using a small safety pin or a hair slide. Press flat with the seam underneath. Applique this strip. Prepare and applique the

---

SHOPPING LIST

2 yd / 1.80 m unbleached calico (sufficient for picture and frame)

For the picture:
½ yd / 45 cm of blue striped cotton fabric
10 in / 25 cm printed cotton for bias strips
cotton scraps for the applique
1 oblong 17 x 15 in / 43 x 38 cm lightweight wadding
1 oblong 17 x 15 in / 43 x 38 cm muslin
13 small old-fashioned buttons (mother-of-pearl and coloured)
toning thread for applique and quilting
strong thread or crochet cotton for lacing picture
gold permanent fabric paint
1 oblong 15 x 13½ in / 38 x 34 cm of mounting card
freezer paper

For the frame:
1 oblong 25 x 23 in / 64 x 58 cm medium-weight polyester wadding / batting
1 oblong 25 x 23 in / 64 x 58 cm muslin
toning quilting thread
gold, bronze and pale yellow permanent fabric paint
oiled manilla paper or acetate
2 oblongs 20½ x 19 in / 52 x 48 cm mounting card
2 1 in / 25 mm brass curtain rings
2 adhesive Velcro tabs
cord for hanging
1 small curved needle (optional)

The appliqued and quilted picture in its frame measures
21 x 19¼ in / 53 x 49 cm. The background of the picture
is embellished with some gold stencilling and old-
fashioned buttons. The stencilled and quilted calico
frame is a project in its own right, perfect for a mirror or
an old photograph.

'leaf' shapes (4 each of Nos. 10. and 11.), following the same method as for the central motif. Remove the freezer paper. Stitch on the buttons.

6. Out of the muslin, cut an oblong 17 x 15 in / 43 x 38 cm. Lay the piece of wadding / batting over it and then the picture, face up. Tack / baste together. Hand-quilt (see instructions on page 121). The quilting lines follow the outlines of the appliqued shapes. Those that do not, can be traced with a pale quilting pencil.

7. Centre the quilted picture over the cardboard mount. Pin into place or attach with masking tape. Lace 1 side first, then the other. Mitre the corners (see **diagrams** opposite). The picture is now ready to be framed.

8. **The picture frame**. Out of the calico, cut 2 oblongs 25 x 23 in / 64 x 58 cm. To 'age' the calico, wash and rinse it well in hot water, then soak it for 30 minutes in strong tea (2 tea bags to a pint / ½ litre of water). Rinse in cold water, dry and press.

9. Enlarge and repeat the pattern on page 12. Transfer the stencil design on to a piece of manilla paper or acetate. On 1 of the oblongs of calico, mark the outline of the frame. Using gold paint, stencil the pattern over the frame area. When dry, use the same stencil, shifting it slightly to one side, and go lightly over the pattern, using bronze paint on the flower and pale yellow on the leaves. This produces a shadow effect. Allow to dry. Fix, following the manufacturer's instructions.

10. Transfer the quilting pattern on to the stencilled frame. Place the piece of muslin on the table, the oblong of wadding / batting over it and then the frame, face up. Tack / baste together. Hand-quilt as explained in paragraph 6.

11. Take 1 of the oblongs of cardboard. Cut out the centre, leaving a frame 3 in / 8 cm wide all round. Lay the quilted panel over the cardboard frame and pin in position. Mitre the corners. Cut out the centre of the fabric panel, as shown in **diagram d**. and pull around each side of the frame. Lace each side of the frame as explained in paragraph 7.

12. To make the backing of the frame, cover the 2nd cardboard oblong with calico, lacing as before and mitring the corners. Sew the 2 curtain rings securely (especially if you are framing a mirror) about ⅓ of the way down the back of the frame. Place the frame and the backing, wrong sides together. Hold with pins. Attach them, using ladder stitch (see **diagram 4**. on page 110). A small curved needle is useful for this work. Leave the top of the frame open. Insert the appliqued picture or the mirror. Slip-stitch the top edge.

Diagram d. *The fabric is pulled around each side of the frame. The flaps are then laced firmly into place.*

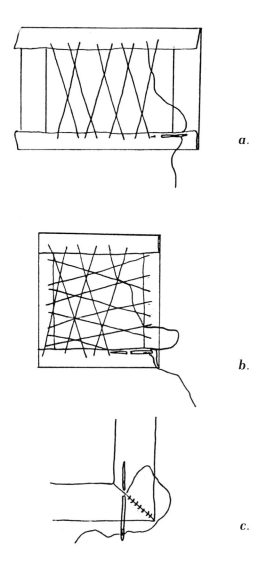

a.

b.

c.

Diagrams a. and b. show the stages of lacing both sides of the fabric over the cardboard backing. The corners are then mitred as in c.

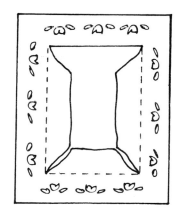

d.

c.

2.

3.

1.

4.

9.

5.

d.

8.

a.

7.

6.

b.

11.

10.

A quarter section of the frame

Enlarge all the elements on this page by 220%. The shapes must be appliqued in the numbered sequence. The broken lines represent quilting lines.

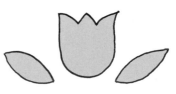

The stencil design

GEOMETRIC WALLHANGING

Jill Essery

This piece is composed of 6 blocks featuring different techniques, but related in colour and forming geometric patterns. Each block is a complete unit, independently lined and quilted, joined together with an insertion stitch to create a modern abstract composition. The choice of colours and patterns is important, contrasting dark and vibrant plain colours with bold stripes and checks.

The seam allowance for the patchwork, unless otherwise stated, is ¼ in / 6 mm.

1. **Block A. – Japanese wrapped and folded patchwork**. Refer to general instructions on page 118. Enlarge the templates on page 18. Use the larger circle to cut 4 cream-coloured shapes. Use the inner circle to cut 1 'ironing' card. Cut 4 4 in / 10 cm squares out of wadding / batting, and 8 of striped fabric (4 along the stripes and 4 across. Also cut 8 plain squares. Prepare the 4 squares as shown on page 118. (The line of black stitching in effect quilts each square.) Put to one side.

2. **The background to block A.** Out of calico cut 1 14 in / 35.5 cm square. Mark centre lines horizontally, vertically and diagonally with a ruler and pencil. Out of 1 of the printed fabrics, cut 1 8½ in / 21.5 cm square. Tack / baste it centrally over the calico. Out of the check material, cut 2 strips 1⅜ x 8½ in / 3.5 x 21.5 cm. Machine-stitch them to the top and bottom of the printed square. Press. Measure 1 of the long dimensions and cut 2 strips to that length and 1⅜ in / 3.5 cm wide. Machine-stitch to the sides of the square. Press.

3. **The outer border**. Measure 1 side of the square and cut 4 strips to that length and 1¾ in / 4.5 cm wide. Cut 4 1¾ in / 4.5 cm yellow squares. Machine-stitch 1 strip to the top and 1 to the bottom of the panel. Join the yellow squares to both ends of the 2 remaining strips. Machine-stitch along the other 2 sides of the panel. Couch narrow red ribbon over the join between the check border and the outer striped one.

4. Attach the 4 Japanese folded patches (see 1. above) to the background of the panel using a few stitches at each corner. Cut 2 2 in / 5 cm black squares. Machine-stitch around 3 sides, trim corners and turn right side out. Slip-stitch opening. Press. Cut 2 1¾ in / 4.5 cm yellow squares. Make up as before. Cut 1 1 in / 2.5 cm square out of contrasting

SHOPPING LIST

¾ yd / 70 cm black polycotton sheeting, 90 in / 228 cm wide
¾ yd / 70 cm ivory-coloured cotton, 45 in / 112 cm wide
½ yd / 45 cm each of 8 different coloured cotton fabrics, 36 in / 90 cm wide (to include narrow and wider striped fabrics, small checks, spotted and bright plain contrasting fabrics)
1 yd / 90 cm of white calico
¾ yd / 70 cm lightweight wadding / batting, 39 in / 100 cm wide
1 small piece of paper-backed fusible web
2 large toning wooden beads or large domed fabric-covered buttons
2 yd / 1.80 m of narrow red ribbon
1 hank of black DMC coton perlé No. 5
1 steel ruler
quilting pencil
1 crewel needle
1 hanging pole

The sketch below shows the position of the individual blocks which form the hanging. Each is identified by a letter.

13

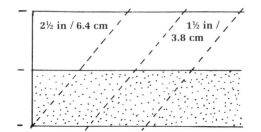

Diagram 1. 1 ivory strip and 1 black, 1½ in / 3.8 cm wide, have been stitched together. This band is folded in half and cut across, along the dotted lines, 1½ in / 3.8 cm apart to obtain black and white strips which mirror each other.

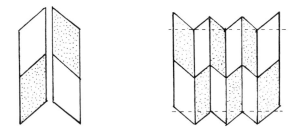

Diagram 2. Arrange pairs, reversing the colours as shown. Join together. Trim off the points along the dotted lines to obtain straight edges.

Opposite page. The finished wallhanging measures 36 x 24 in / 90 x 61 cm.

This sketch shows how the small triangular inserts are produced. Cut diagonally to obtain 2 triangles.

fabric and 1 out of paper-backed fusible web. Attach the web to the back of the square, according to the manufacturer's instructions, and press to fix this contrasting square in the centre of the yellow one. The yellow square forms a diamond over the black one. Fix them to the centre of the Japanese patches, with a large single cross stitch.

5. **Lining the block**. Out of the black fabric cut 6 squares to the same size as that of the completed block, then cut 6 squares of lightweight wadding / batting. Tack / baste 1 of the squares of wadding / batting to the back of the completed block. Place block, right sides together, over the lining. Machine-stitch all round, leaving a 4 in / 10 cm gap for turning. Trim excess wadding / batting from the seam. Turn right side out. Slip-stitch opening.

6. **Block B**. The ivory and black striped pattern at the centre of the block is made up of a variation of seminole patchwork in which 2 contrasting strips are machine-stitched together, cut and reassembled to produce a geometric pattern. Cut and machine-stitch 1 strip of black and 1 of ivory, 1½ x 55 in / 3.8 x 140 cm. Fold in half and cut according to **diagram 1**. opposite. Reverse the colours and join the pieces as in **diagram 2**. Refer to No. 4 of general instructions on page 116. Draw a line and trim off the points as shown. The rest of the block is made up of strip patchwork. Starting on the right of the seminole, cut 2 strips of striped fabric 1 x 13 in / 2.5 x 33 cm. Cut 2 1½ x 13 in / 3.8 x 33 cm out of contrasting fabrics and 1 in black. Cut 1 large black strip 2¼ x 13 in / 5.5 x 33 cm. Attach all these strips to the seminole with the large black strip on the outside (refer to picture of hanging). Working from the left of the seminole, cut 3 strips 1¼ in / 3.2 cm, ¾ in / 2 cm, 1½ in / 3.8 cm wide respectively, all 13 in / 33 cm long. Assemble on to the seminole band.

7. **Triangular inserts**. Cut 2 2½ in / 6.5 cm squares (same or differently coloured). Machine-stitch all round. Cut in half diagonally. (See sketch opposite.) Turn right side out. Press.

8. Prepare 2 triangles as in 7. above. Stagger them slightly and pin them to the edge of the last strip. Cut the final black strip 3 x 13 in / 7.5 x 33 cm. Machine-stitch to the left of the panel. Press, pushing the triangular insert over the black strip. Proceed as in paragraph 4. Trim off excess fabric and wadding / batting.

9. **Block C**. The ivory and black pattern 'Tree Everlasting' is made up of seamed patchwork. Use the template on page 18 to cut 8 black and 7 ivory shapes. Join 5 pieces of alternate colours end to end to make a strip. Repeat twice and join the 3 strips together to make the pattern. Cut 3 strips ¾ in / 2 cm, 1⅜ in / 3.5 cm, 3½ in / 9 cm (black) respectively, all 13 in / 33 cm long. Make 3 triangular inserts as in paragraph 7. Stagger 2 of them. Pin in position next to the black stripe. Assemble as before. Press. Starting from the left of the ivory

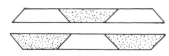

Block C. This sketch shows how to position the black and ivory shapes to produce the 'Tree Everlasting' pattern, using the template on page 18.

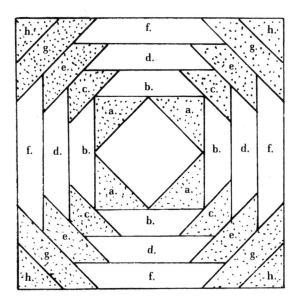

*Diagram 3. The working sequence, starting from the centre square. On page 18 you will find the 8 templates, marked from **a.** to **h.**, which, together with the centre square, form the pineapple pattern.*

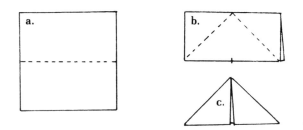

Block E. These sketches show how to fold the components of the folded star.

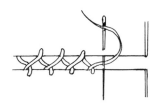

Diagram 4. Joining the blocks, using an insertion stitch and coton perlé.

/ black band, prepare 1 ¾ in / 2 cm wide strip (cut on the bias out of striped material), 1 1 in / 2.5 cm, 3 1¼ in / 3.2 cm (1 is black), 1 4 in / 10 cm. Assemble and line as in paragraph 5. Trim off excess fabric and wadding / batting.

10. **Block D.** The main feature is a square of pineapple log cabin. Enlarge the templates on page 18, as instructed, and cut out of your selected fabrics, contrasting light and dark shades, as marked. **Diagram 3** shows the working sequence. The general instructions for pineapple log cabin appear on page 117. I added 4 triangular inserts (striped fabric) around the centre square before joining templates a). Refer to paragraph 7. Build up the block as in the general instruction until you are about to join h) to g), at the outer corners. Here I inserted elongated triangles. Use the template on page 18, cutting 4 striped and 4 plain. Machine-stitch 1 plain to 1 striped triangle, along the 2 long dimensions. Turn right side out, clip corners and press. Place pineapple block right side up on the table. Pin triangle, striped side up over g), matching raw edges. Machine-stitch h) in the usual way. Repeat for the other corners. Press these 4 seams towards the centre of the block. The points of the triangles will eventually be attached by a couple of stitches so that they curl towards the centre. Pin them back for the moment to avoid catching them in the sewing. Prepare 4 striped and 4 yellow triangles (see paragraph 7). Attach the 4 striped ones to the centre of f), on the outside of the pineapple block.

11. Measure 1 side of the block. Cut 2 strips to that length, 1½ in / 3.8 cm wide. Attach to the top and bottom of the square. Measure 1 of the long dimensions. Cut 2 strips to that length and 1½ in / 3.8 cm wide. Machine-stitch. Proceed the same way for the check border, cutting the strip to the new length and 1¼ in / 3.2 cm wide. Attach the 4 yellow triangles prepared in 10. above to the centre of the check strips. The outer border with purple corners is 1¾ in / 4.5 cm wide. Proceed as in paragraph 3. Insert 1 large bead or have a domed button covered in toning fabric. Attach it to the very centre of the block, under the triangular inserts. Finish the block as described in paragraph 5.

12. **Block E.** The main feature of this block is a folded star. Turn to instructions on page 115. Out of the black polycotton, cut 1 12 in / 30.5 cm square. Use a pencil or a fine gold marker to draw the lines as indicated. The version in the hanging consists of 7 rows. **Row 1.:** cut 4 pieces 2 x 2½ in / 50 x 62 mm. **Rows 2 and 3**: cut 8 pieces each of 2 different colours, 2½ x 3 in / 62 x 76 mm. **Rows 4, 5 and 6**: cut 16 pieces each of 3 different colours, 2½ x 3 in / 62 x 76 mm. **Row 7**: 16 pieces, 3 x 3½ in / 76 x 90 mm. Cut 8 more pieces of the same colour and size to complete the corners and make up a square shape. Refer to paragraph 11, to join the check border, which is 1¼ in / 31 mm wide. Repeat for the narrow pink border which is ¾ in / 20 mm wide. Prepare 4 striped and 4 plain triangular inserts as in paragraph 7, and join centrally to the pink strip.

13. The outer border is made up of strips of seminole patchwork. Refer to instructions on page 116. Cut 2 black and 1 ivory strips, 1½ x 12 in / 4 x 30 cm. Join, with the ivory strip in the centre. Cut and reassemble, as instructed. Snip off the points to get straight edges. Repeat 3 times. Measure the width of 1 of the prepared strips and cut 4 yellow squares to that dimension. Assemble this outer border as in paragraph 3. The yellow squares have been decorated with 2 contrasting diamonds each, applied with paper-backed fusible web, as for the centre of block A. Couch a length of narrow red ribbon over the join between the central star and the check border. Insert a wooden bead or button in the centre, as for block D.

14. **Block F.** The ivory and black checkerboard band is seminole patchwork. Cut 3 black and 3 ivory strips 1½ x 10 in / 3.8 x 25 cm. Take 1 ivory strip and machine-stitch 1 black strip at either side. Take 1 black strip and machine-stitch 1 ivory strip at either side. Measure and cut at 1½ in / 3.8 cm intervals. Prepare 3 triangular inserts (you may have some left from before). Alternate and machine-stitch the short strips of seminole to create a checkerboard effect, slipping the triangular inserts between the rows.

15. Starting from the right of the seminole band, cut 3 strips (1 black) 1¼ / 3.2 cm wide and 1 large black strip 2½ / 6.4 cm wide – all 13 in / 33 cm long. Machine-stitch as before. From the left of the seminole band, cut 1 strip 1¼ / 3.2 cm wide, 3 strips ⅞ in / 2.2 cm (the striped one was cut on the bias), 1 1½ in / 3.8 cm wide. The final black strip is 4¼ in / 11 cm wide. All the strips are 13 in / 33 cm long. Assemble as before. Cut 1 4 in / 10 cm square of striped fabric and fold in the same way as the components of the folded star in block E. Attach to the base of block F. Finish off the block as in paragraph 5.

16. **Joining the blocks.** Arrange the blocks over the table, in the correct order. Any small discrepancies in size between the blocks can be compensated by adjusting the length of the insertion stitch, which is worked with a crewel needle, using coton perlé (see **diagram 4.** on opposite page). Attach loops (concealed or exposed) at the back of the hanging and hang from a pole.

*Above right. Block **A**. One patch of Japanese folded patchwork. Note the yellow square, with the superimposed pink one, held to the piece by a large cross stitch.*

*Middle picture. Block **D**. This detail shows one of the elongated triangles mentioned in paragraph 10. The points have been attached with a stitch to curl towards the centre.*

*Opposite. Block **E**. Detail from the folded star.*

Enlarge everything on this page 200%.

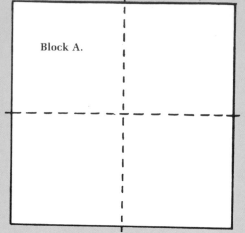

Block A.

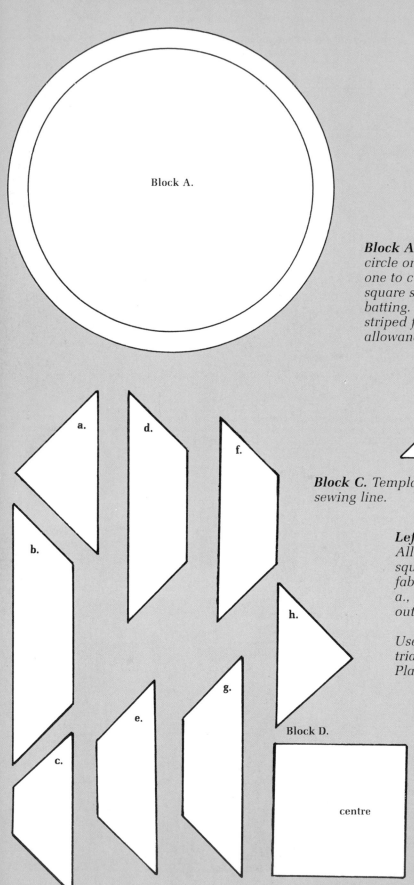

Block A.

Block A. *Japanese folded patchwork. Use the outer circle on the left to cut the white fabric. Use the inner one to cut the ironing template out of stiff card. Use the square shape above to cut the piece of wadding / batting. Use the smaller squares to cut the plain and striped fabric, adding ¼ in / 6 mm for the seam allowance.*

Block C. *Template for 'Tree Everlasting'. The dotted line is the sewing line.*

Left. *Block **D.** Templates for pineapple log cabin. All include 1/4 in / 6 mm seam allowance. Use the square to cut 1 for the centre out of a contrasting fabric. Cut 4 each of the other 8 shapes as follows: a., c., e., g. and h. out of a dark fabric; b., d. and f. out of a light-coloured one.*

Use the triangle below to produce the 'elongated triangles' mentioned at the end of paragraph 10. Place the vertical line along the grain of the fabric.

Block D.

centre

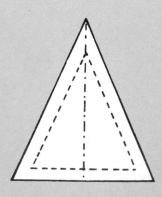

Block D.

One of a pair of 'heart' cushions, made by Gisela Thwaites. This one reflects her love of Indian embroidery and colours. A couple of peacock 'eyes' are combined with beading and form a salient feature in this piece. The detail below and the diagram on page 22 show you how it is done. The picture also shows how simple embroidery, highlighted with tiny beads, can produce a richly textured surface.

TWIN 'HEART' CUSHIONS

Gisela Thwaites

The same pattern and method are used to produce a pair of cushions, but with quite different results. The example opposite has a Victorian mood, while the turquoise cushion on page 19 illustrates my love of Indian embroidery, textiles and jewel-like colour combinations. These are good projects with which to practise my special brand of embellishment.

General principles. I have used crazy patchwork in all the projects included in this book. This enables me to make use of the tiniest scraps of fabric as I don't have to worry about grain direction. I like to mix silk and cotton, sateen, velvet, brocade, linen, damask, bits of leather, lace etc. I am a great collector of 'bits' and am always looking for intriguing buttons, oddments of lace, old beads, scraps of ribbon. I incorporate shishas – the mirror pieces used in the traditional embroidery in many parts of India. I use simple embroidery – herringbone, feather, chain and running stitches – often embroidering the patches first, then appliqueing them.

1. **The heart panel**. Assemble your scraps of fabric and decide on the colour scheme. Enlarge the template on page 22.

2 Fold and press the piece of foundation material in half and half again to mark the middle. Lay the heart template in the centre of the foundation material and draw out the outline. Mark the top and the bottom of the heart shape with a pin. Turn the material over and draw the outline of the heart again, in exactly the same position as before. You will find this helpful when the panel has been covered with patches: it will give the true shape of the heart when you want to outline it with embroidery or braid.

3. Cut up the heart template into its individual numbered shapes. In the finished heart motif the pieces overlap each other like scales. The curved arrows on the template indicate where the edge of the fabric is coming over the next patch, and is appliqued with slip stitches. Pin or tack / baste the numbered paper shapes *on top* of the selected fabrics, making sure that the colours and patterns work harmoniously with one another. Cut the fabric pieces, including a ⅝ in / 15 mm seam allowance. Turn over the edges on the seam lines with curved arrows and press them. Position piece 1., then piece 2., allowing the folded edge of 1. to overlap the edge of 2. Pin or tack / baste and continue until all the pieces are in position. Slip-stitch along the

seams. Leave the outside edges of the pieces to lie flat over the heart outline. Remove paper templates and any tacking / basting. Press. Turn the work over and run a line of tacking / basting along the heart outline.

4. Following instructions for crazy patchwork on page 113, fill in the remaining space on the panel. Use narrow, straight shapes, allowing them to radiate from the heart shape. This makes it stand out. The fabric pieces should overlay the outer edges of the heart by at least ⅝ in / 15 mm. When the panel is full, turn under the edges of the pieces along the heart shape, using the line of tacking / basting as a guide.

This version of the 'heart' cushion has a Victorian feel, due chiefly to the choice of colours and materials. (Cotton fabrics and Liberty prints can be 'aged' by soaking in strong tea for a while before use.) Old-fashioned braid and buttons are combined with beading and simple embroidery.

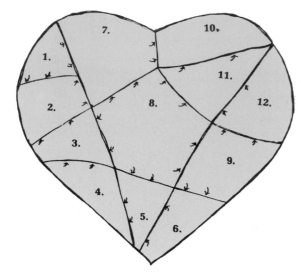

Enlarge this template 400% on the photocopier. Remember to applique the patches in the numbered sequence.

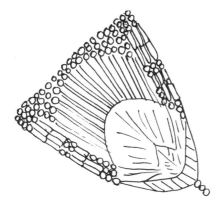

Lay the peacock 'eye' on a piece of one-sided adhesive paper. Trim into shape and attach to the cushion with a little fabric adhesive. When it is dry, use peacock blue and iridescent bugles and beads to complete the motif.

Below. *Some of the embroidery stitches used on the cushions. On the right is an assortment of beads and a 'silk' knot.*

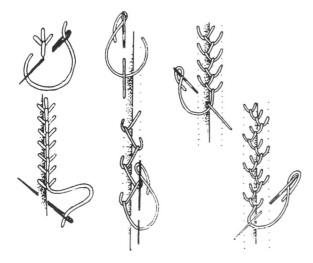

Press. Now starts the fun part! Use embroidery and metallic threads and work herringbone or feather stitches over the outlines of the patchwork patches. Pick out the beads. Outline printed patterns with stitching. Make little flower shapes using grouped sequins and combining them with beads, bugles and French knots. The turquoise cushion incorporates 2 peacock eyes, appliqued and ornamented with beads (see sketch). Apply shishas (see method on page 94), buttons etc. Use your imagination and you'll soon think of ways in which to embellish your work, using the little 'treasures' you collected. Lay the piece of wadding / batting on the table, lay the completed panel, face up, over it and pin together. Use braid to outline the edge of the heart and slip-stitch into position, securing the ends of the braid. Work a few invisible stitches here and there to hold the batting / wadding on to the panel. Trim the edges of the panel down so that it measures 15 in / 38 cm square. This includes a ⅝ in / 15 mm seam allowance all round.

5. **Making up the cushion**. Cut 4 strips of plain furnishing fabric 23¾ x 5½ in / 600 x 138 mm. Fold one in half to find the centre and mark with a pin. Mark the centre of one side of the patchwork panel with a pin. Lay 1 of the strips over 1 side of the border over the panel, right sides together, matching the pins. Pin together and machine-stitch. Repeat for the other sides, leaving the ends of the strips loose. To mitre the corners of the border, lay the work flat on the table. Fold the patchwork panel diagonally and run a line of stitching from the corner of the panel to the corner of the border. Repeat on remaining corners. Trim off excess fabric. Press. Outline the edge of the patchwork panel with cord, pushing the ends under the mitred corner, and slip-stitch.

6. Lay the front of the cushion over the furnishing fabric. Cut a square of the same size. Pin, right sides together, and machine-stitch all round, leaving a 13 in / 33 cm opening. Turn the work right side out. Put in the pad. Close the opening and slip-stitch cord along the edge, pushing the ends into the corner of the seam.

Emma sporting the bag made by Jill Essery. (See project on page 64.

CHESSBOARD

Christine Donaldson

(Diagrams not to scale)

1.

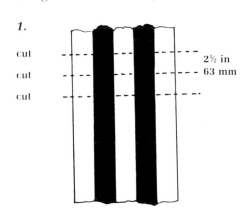

cut

cut

cut

2½ in
63 mm

Below. The checkerboard pattern.
Cut along dotted line.
1a.

The sophisticated appeal of this chessboard comes from its crisp lines and intricate border patterns – different on each side. It will make an elegant gift, attractive enough to hang on the wall when the game is over. I used lightweight, closely woven pure cottons and selected Seminole patchwork, which relies on strong tonal contrasts for its effectiveness. This exciting technique, developed by the Seminole tribe of Native Americans, involves machine-stitching strips of contrasting fabrics, then cutting and rearranging them to form deceptively complex patterns. Basic instructions for Seminole patchwork appear on page 116.

The patchwork seam allowance is ¼ in / 6 mm. Whenever possible in this project, press the seams towards the darker fabric. This will not always be possible and a little show-through is unavoidable, but it won't matter, so long as the seams are neat and even.

1. **Black and white squares.** Cut 4 strips of plain black cotton and 5 of cream cotton, each 2½ x 21 in / 63 x 533 mm. Machine-stitch, alternating the colours, starting and finishing with the cream. Press the seams towards the black fabric. (See **diagrams 1.** and **1a.** opposite.) Cut across the resulting 'fabric' into strips 2½ in / 63 mm wide, rearrange into the checkerboard pattern. Pin and stitch together. Trim off the excess cream squares, leaving the required seam allowance. Press the seams.

2. **The narrow inner border.** Join strips of 2 of your contrasting patterned fabrics 2 x 90 in / 5 x 229 cm (this is the total length but it can be made in more than 1 section, as it will get cut up in any case). Press. Cut into pieces 1 in / 25 mm wide. Reposition pieces, machine-stitch. Press and trim. (See **diagrams 2.** and **2a.** on page 25.)

3. **Mounting the inner border.** Cut 2 strips of the prepared border to the same length as the sides of the central panel (black and white squares). Pin and machine-stitch to opposite sides. Press seams outwards. Cut strips for the 2 remaining sides, remembering that these are longer than the previous 2, as they now include the width of the border. Pin, stitch and press seams.

4. **Plain cream border.** Cut a strip of plain cream fabric 1 x 74 in / 2.5 x 188 cm (total length – can be joined). Repeat stage 3 to make and attach this second border.

5. **Side borders**. See **diagrams 3.** to **6a.** on page 27, which explain how the 4 patterns are made up. Measurements are given, but due to the inherent elasticity of Seminole patchwork, it is wise to check the length of the prepared strips and to adjust them accordingly.

6. The 4 completed side borders should be trimmed to measure 3½ in / 88 mm in width. Attach 2 opposite sides as described in stage 3.

7. To complete the side borders, measure along the 2 lengths of the narrow cream border and add ½ in / 12 mm for seams. Cut the 2 remaining bands of Seminole patchwork to this length. Cut and attach 2 cream cotton squares 3½ in / 88 mm to either end. Press seams. Pin and stitch these 2 borders, carefully aligning the seams at the corners.

8. Place the piece of heavyweight sew-in interlining (24 in / 61 cm square) on the table and lay the completed work over it, facing up. Pin and tack / baste the central checkerboard panel into position, then quilt 'in the ditch' with invisible nylon thread, along the rows of squares, in both directions (see basic instructions on page 121).

9. Fold back 2 opposite border panels and place a strip of polyester wadding / batting to lie neatly between them and the interlining and flush to the edge of the checkerboard and the outer edge of the borders. Repeat for the other sides, butting the ends of the wadding / batting up to the first strips of wadding / batting.

10. Fold the borders back into place and pin and tack / baste the 3 layers (patchwork, wadding, interlining) together. Using the invisible thread, quilt 'in the ditch' along the 2 narrow borders and the corner squares.

11. Lay the square of backing fabric, wrong side up, on the table, lay the quilted chessboard, right side up, over it and pin into place.

12. Trim the wadding / batting, interlining and backing fabric exactly level with the patchwork top and tack / baste all 4 layers together around the outer edge.

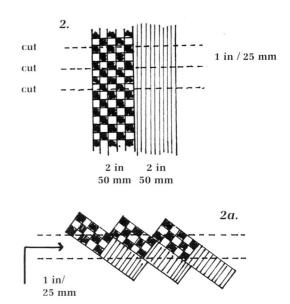

2.

cut

cut

cut

1 in / 25 mm

2 in
50 mm

2 in
50 mm

2a.

1 in/
25 mm

Overleaf. *The finished chessboard measures 23½ in / 60 cm square.*

Below. *Details from the corners of the chessboard, showing the narrow inner border and the 4 different patterns contained in the side borders.*

13. **Binding and mitring the work**. (See basic instructions on page 122.) Cut a strip of black cotton 3 x 100 in / 7.5 x 254 cm. To obtain the total length, join sections with a diagonal seam to distribute the bulk. Bind and mitre the corners of the border.

The diagrams on this page are not to scale.

*The 4th border (**diagrams 4.** to **4b.**) combines 2 different patterns.*

*Note that in **diagrams 3., 4., 5.** and **6.** only the width of the original strips of fabric is given. In each case, their length should be 34 in / 86 cm.*

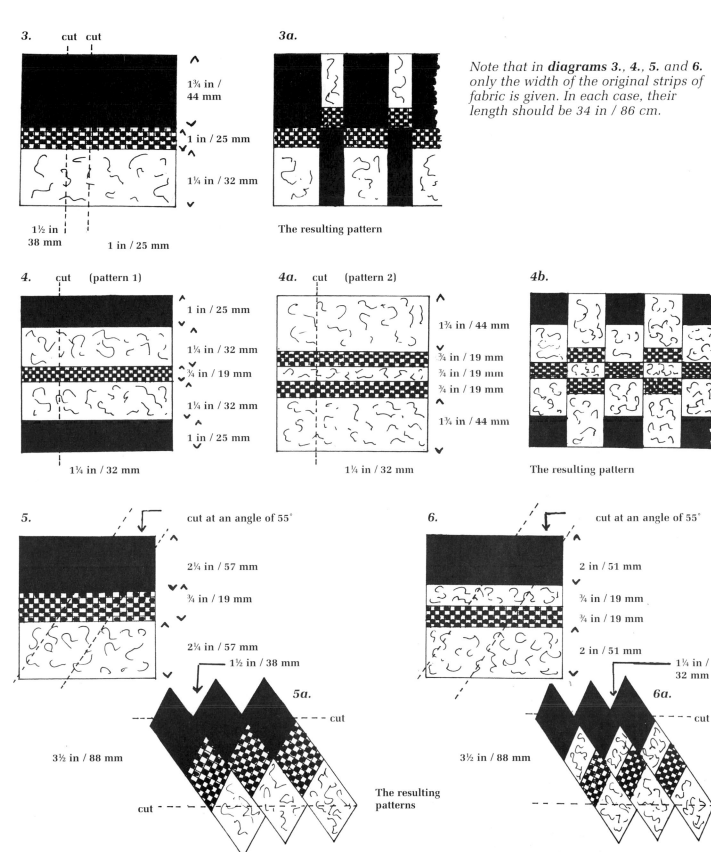

3.   cut   cut

1¾ in / 44 mm

1 in / 25 mm

1¼ in / 32 mm

1½ in / 38 mm

1 in / 25 mm

3a.

The resulting pattern

4.   cut   (pattern 1)

1 in / 25 mm

1¼ in / 32 mm

¾ in / 19 mm

1¼ in / 32 mm

1 in / 25 mm

1¼ in / 32 mm

4a.   cut   (pattern 2)

1¾ in / 44 mm

¾ in / 19 mm

¾ in / 19 mm

¾ in / 19 mm

1¾ in / 44 mm

1¼ in / 32 mm

4b.

The resulting pattern

5.

cut at an angle of 55°

2¼ in / 57 mm

¾ in / 19 mm

2¼ in / 57 mm

1½ in / 38 mm

3½ in / 88 mm

cut

cut

5a.

The resulting patterns

6.

cut at an angle of 55°

2 in / 51 mm

¾ in / 19 mm

¾ in / 19 mm

2 in / 51 mm

1¼ in / 32 mm

3½ in / 88 mm

cut

6a.

SAMPLER CUSHION

Gilly Wraight

The finished cushion measures 20 in / 51 cm square. The detail shown below displays some of the simple hand and machine embroidery which embellishes the cushion.

This colourful cushion has a central panel, made up of 4 blocks of American seamed patchwork. Each block is made up of different geometrical shapes and each has its own colour scheme. You'll need 12 different 'related' fabrics. This cushion was to some extent inspired by my discovery of an exciting mottled cotton material which was available in a large range of graduated colours. I found it at a quilt exhibition, where many specialist suppliers had assembled a mouth-watering array of fabrics. I succumbed! The resulting cushion will complement traditional as well as crisp modern furnishings. It is embellished with a mixture of machine and hand embroidery.

1. Enlarge the 6 templates at the top of page 31, as instructed. Make a master of each and number them carefully.

2. Out of the light blue fabric, cut a strip 15 x 5 in / 38 x 13 cm. Repeat in light green, bright red and dark pink fabrics. Lay to one side. Cut 1 5 in / 13 cm square out of the dark blue fabric, 1 orange, 1 dark green and 1 dark red. These 4 strips and 4 squares will eventually form the border of the cushion.

3. Refer to the photograph opposite and to the diagrams on page 30.

   a) **Red / orange block**. Use template 6. Cut 1 yellow and 1 orange square. Cut 2 squares of wadding / batting.

   Use template 2. Cut 2 bright red and 2 orange triangles.

   b) **Green block**. Use template 5. and cut 1 dark green large triangle. Cut 1 of wadding / batting.

   Use template 2, and cut 1 light green, 2 middle green and 1 dark green triangles.

   c) **Pink / red block**. Use template 3. and cut 2 light pink, 2 dark pink, 2 light red and 2 dark red triangles.

   Use template 4. and cut 1 light pink, 1 dark pink, 2 light red and 1 dark red squares. Cut 2 of wadding / batting.

   d) **Blue block**. Use template 1. and cut 1 light blue square. Cut 1 of wadding / batting.

   Use template 2. and cut 4 dark blue triangles.

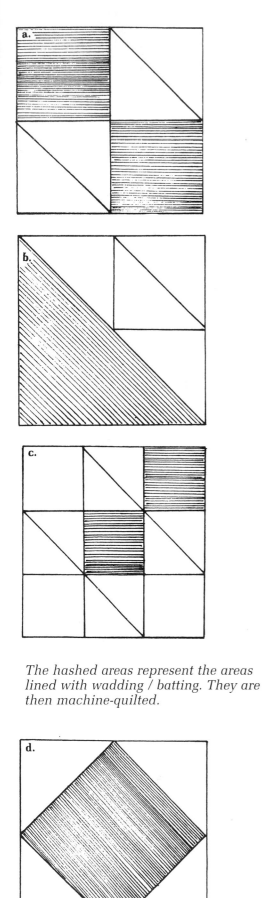

The hashed areas represent the areas lined with wadding / batting. They are then machine-quilted.

4. **Assembling the blocks**. Refer to instructions for American seamed patchwork on page 114.

   a) **Red / orange block**. The diagram on the left shows that the 2 square patches are lined with wadding / batting. This gives texture and makes these 2 patches stand out. Put the fabric patches, face up, on the wadding / batting. Tack / baste. Machine-quilt a set of lines over each square in toning or contrasting thread (refer to picture of cushion). Add a few lines of herringbone stitches. Join 1 red to 1 orange triangle to make square. Repeat. Join with the quilted orange and yellow squares to make the first block.

   b) **Green block**. Attach wadding / batting to the dark green triangle, as explained in a) above. Machine-stitch straight quilting lines and add a little hand embroidery: running stitch, French knots etc. Join the light and dark green triangles to make a square. Attach the 2 medium green triangles and join the resulting triangle to the quilted one.

   c) **Pink / red block**. Attach wadding / batting to the light pink and the dark red squares. Machine-quilt. Join the triangles to make squares, assemble as explained above and finish the block, adding hand embroidery. In this case, I used 6 strands of embroidery cotton and couched them with toning thread.

   d) **Blue block**. Attach wadding / batting to the large pale blue square. Machine-quilt. Use coton à broder to work lengths of herringbone, cross stitch and running stitch. Assemble the block and work 1 spider in each dark-blue triangle.

5. Join the 4 blocks together. Press. Take the pale green long strip you cut, as explained in paragraph 2. Lay it, right sides together, over the top edge of the patchwork panel. Pin and machine-stitch. Cut excess fabric if necessary. Take the blue strip, check its length against the right-hand edge of the patchwork panel and trim excess fabric if necessary. Join the dark green and dark blue squares at either end of the strip. Align the seams at the corners of the patchwork panel. Pin and machine-stitch. Repeat for the remaining 2 sides. Press. Measure the width of the border. It should be 4 in / 10 cm wide all round, which includes a ⅝ in / 15 mm seam allowance. Trim excess fabric if necessary. Lay the back of the cushion face up on the table. Put the front of the cushion face down, over it. Trim excess fabric off the back of the cushion if necessary. Machine-stitch ⅝ in / 15 mm away from the edge, leaving a 10 in / 26 cm opening for turning the cushion right side out. Insert the pad. Slip-stitch the opening.

The diagrams on the left show the 4 individual blocks, their make-up and the areas lined with wadding / batting, prior to quilting.

30

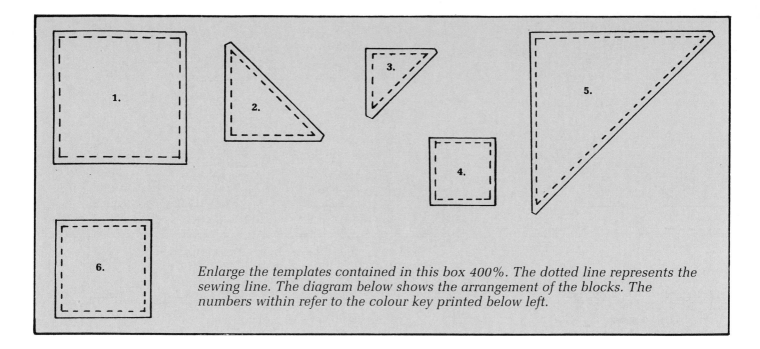

Enlarge the templates contained in this box 400%. The dotted line represents the sewing line. The diagram below shows the arrangement of the blocks. The numbers within refer to the colour key printed below left.

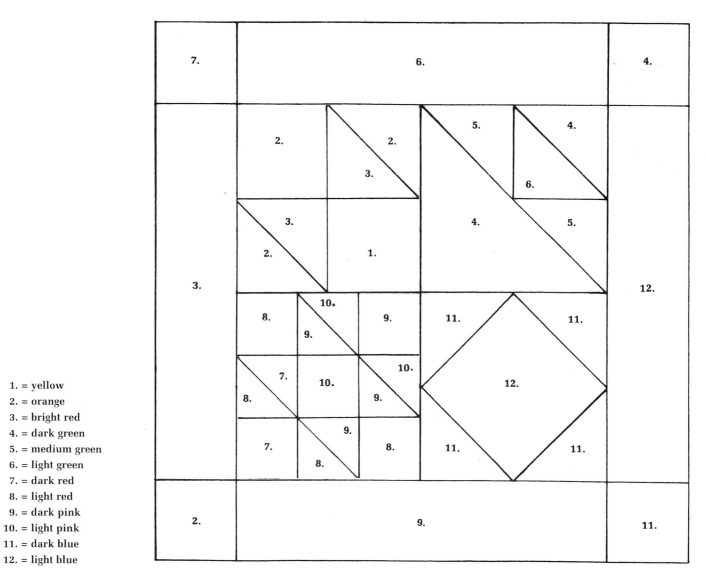

1. = yellow
2. = orange
3. = bright red
4. = dark green
5. = medium green
6. = light green
7. = dark red
8. = light red
9. = dark pink
10. = light pink
11. = dark blue
12. = light blue

STRIP PATCHWORK EVENING JACKET

❧

Jill Essery

The colour scheme for this garment was inspired by the dramatically striped marble work found in the Gothic cathedrals of central Italy. The lapels are cord-quilted in a geometric pattern. The back of the garment is of black silk, quilted vertically. Piped seams continue the striped theme.

1. Enlarge the pattern pieces on pages 38-39, as instructed. Cut 2 of the *front of the jacket* out of the soft interlining, transferring notches. Set aside.

2. **Strip patchwork.** It adds interest to the garment if the strips are of different widths. For the 1st front cut 12 pale grey strips 1⅛ in x 36 in / 2.8 x 90 cm and 2 1½ x 36 in / 3.8 x 90 cm. Cut 2 strips of mid-grey 1¼ x 36 in / 3.2 x 90 cm and 2 1 x 36 in / 2.5 x 90 cm. Cut 2 strips of black 1 x 36 in / 2.5 x 90 cm and 3 strips 1¼ x 36 in / 3.2 x 90 cm. Cut 4 strips of bronze 1¼ x 36 in / 3.2 x 90 cm. Cut 1 strip of striped 1⅜ x 36 in / 3.5 x 90 cm and 1 1 x 36 in / 2.5 x 90 cm. See jacket caption for the colour arrangement. Join the strips. The seam allowance for the patchwork is ¼ in / 6 mm. Repeat in reverse for the opposite front of the jacket. Press all the seams in the same direction.

3. Place the 2 pieces of made-up 'fabric' wrong sides together on the table. Place the pattern of the jacket front over it. The lapel edge of the pattern should run parallel with the 1st pale grey stripe. It will *not* reach up to the edge, though, as the total width of the front of the garment will be made up by the width of the applied lapel. The grain line on the pattern must align with the stripes. Transfer shoulder and sleeve notches. Place each jacket front, right sides facing, over its interlining (cut in 1. above), matching shoulder and sleeve notches. Tack / baste together.

4. **Back of the jacket.** Place the paper pattern over the *folded* black silk. Cut 1, adding an extra 1 in / 25 mm to each side seam, to compensate for the quilting. Transfer notches and darts. Run a row of long tacking / basting stitches along the fabric fold to mark the centre of the back. Cut 1 of wadding / batting and 1 of butter muslin (to the same size as the silk). Do not transfer markings on these. Machine-stitch the small neckline darts on the black silk. Use the quilting pencil to rule vertical quilting guidelines, 2¼ in / 55 mm apart, working from the marked central line of tacking / basting. Place the muslin piece on the table, then the piece of wadding / batting and finally the back of the jacket, right

SHOPPING LIST

3 yd / 2.70 m black dupion or other medium-weight silk, 44 in / 112 cm wide*
1 yd / 90 cm pale grey silk as above
1 yd / 90 cm mid-grey silk as above
1 yd / 90 cm bronze-coloured silk as above
1 yd / 90 cm thinly striped silk as above
3 yd / 2.70 m contrasting silk for lining as above
1 large toning frog fastening
2 yd / 2 m butter muslin
2 yd / 2 m soft lightweight sew-in interlining *or* soft brushed cotton
Stitch 'n' Tear tear-off backing
1 yd / 90 cm lightweight wadding / batting
1½ yd / 1.40 m piping cord No. 2
4 skeins quilting wool
large tapestry needle or bodkin
black and silver or black / bronze mix machine embroidery thread
toning sewing threads
black coton perlé No. 5
long steel or plastic quilter's ruler
rotary cutter and cutting mat (optional)
quilting pencil

*The quantities stated are sufficient to enable you to cut the silk pieces parallel to the selvedges. Many silks, including dupions, fray less if you cut the strips in this way.

Opposite. The finished evening jacket. The colour arrangement of the strips on the jacket fronts starting from the lapel is: pale grey, bronze, black, mid-grey, striped, pale grey, black, mid-grey, striped, black, bronze, pale grey, black, mid-grey, bronze, pale grey, black, striped, bronze and mid-grey. Distribute the various widths randomly. The jacket is a universal size, made up to a length of 32 in / 80 cm. It is easy to adjust the length of the garment or of the sleeves.

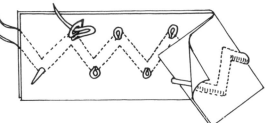

Diagram 1. Cord quilting the chevrons. The wrong side of the work shows quilting wool being inserted between the top fabric and the muslin. Small loops of wool are left at the angles of the pattern.

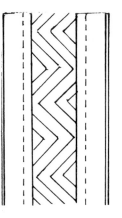

Diagram 2. Piping being attached to the right side of the lapel. The raw edges will then be folded to the back.

Diagrams 3. and 4. In 3. we see the folded raw edges held with a herringbone stitch at the back of the lapel. The next diagram shows the piped lapel.

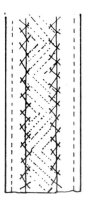

side up. Pin together from the centre outwards. Using machine-metallic thread, machine-quilt along the ruled lines. Check the quilted back against the back paper pattern and trim off excess fabric if necessary. Mark notches again if they have been trimmed off.

5. Join the front to the back of the jacket at the shoulder seams, matching notches. Clip curves. Trim back excess wadding / batting from the seam allowance.

6. **The lapels.** Place the pattern of the front lapel over the *folded* black silk, along the grain of the fabric. Cut. Place the pattern over the Stitch 'n' Tear and cut 2. Repeat with the muslin. Cut 1 of the back of the lapel out of black silk, 1 out of Stitch 'n' Tear and 1 out of muslin.

7. **Cord quilting the lapels.** Transfer the chevron quilting guideline from the lapel pattern pieces on to the Stitch 'n' Tear shapes. Start with the back of the lapel. Place the muslin shape on the table, put the corresponding piece of black silk on top of it and the marked Stitch 'n' Tear uppermost. Machine-stitch along the marked chevron line, using black sewing thread and a medium stitch length. Leave the needle in the fabric when you reach an angle and lift the foot of the machine to turn the fabric. Remove Stitch 'n' Tear. Work the parallel lines of the chevrons, using the width of the machine foot as a guide. Alternatively, mark the lines with a ruler and a quilting pencil. The chevrons should fill the entire shape, *up to the seam allowance.* Repeat for the 2 front lapels. Complete the quilting by inserting quilting wool into the channels, as shown in **diagram 1.** Using a large tapestry needle, insert the wool from the back, pushing the loose weave of the muslin apart to enter and exit the needle. Wherever there is a change of direction, take the wool out to the back surface and re-enter the same hole, leaving a little loop sticking out. Leave a small tail of thread sticking out when starting or finishing a length.

8. **Piping the lapels.** Out of the striped silk, cut bias strips 1½ in / 38 mm wide. Join to make 5 yd /4.50 m. Press in half lengthwise. Pin along each side of the lapels, on the right side, with the folded edge of the piping lying towards the centre, and the raw edges pointing outwards. The finished piping will be ¼ in / 6 mm wide (see **diagram 2.**). Machine-stitch along this seam line, leaving the last 3 in / 75 mm towards the shoulder seam unstitched for the moment. Fold the raw edges of the piping and lapels under. Pin to the wrong side and fix with a row of herringbone stitch (see **diagrams 3. and 4.**). Repeat for the back of the lapels, leaving 3 in / 75 mm unstitched at either end.

9. Tack / baste the front lapels to the front edges of the jacket. The piped lapels should overlap and hide the raw edge of the first silk strip. Top-stitch between the edge of the lapel and the onset of the piping. If it is done exactly in the hollow of the seam, the stitches will be almost invisible.

The remaining 3 in / 75 mm, near the shoulder, should be left unstitched.

10. Attach the edge of the interlining to the back of the lapels with a large herringbone stitch, ensuring it does not show on the right side.

11. **Assembling the lapels**. Pin or tack / baste the front part of the lapels to the back. Pin around the neckline to check that the seams align with the shoulder join of the garment. Adjust if necessary. Unpin the neckline and machine-stitch the fronts to the back of the lapels. Trim away excess quilting wool and muslin from the seam allowance. Open seams flat. Tack / baste to hold. The 3 in / 75 mm of piping left unstitched on either side of the shoulder seam can now be finished off. Pin the bias piping in position, working from the front of the garment. Push the raw edges under. The piping should show neatly at either side. Where 2 ends of piping meet, 1 should overlap the other by ½ in / 15 mm. Fold 1 end under to encase the other neatly and cover all raw edges. Tack / baste the back of the lapel to the back of the jacket. Top-stitch along the hollow of the piping as before.

12. **The sleeves**. Using the paper pattern, cut 2 out of the interlining, transferring the notches. To make the strip patchwork, cut 9 strips of black silk and 9 of pale grey, 2 x 24 in / 5 x 61 cm. Repeat for 2nd sleeve. Join the black and grey strips alternately. Press. Place the 2 pieces of made-up 'fabric' wrong sides together on the table. Place the sleeve paper pattern on top, ensuring the grain marking follows the seam lines of the patchwork. Cut, transferring notches and dots. Tack / baste the sleeves to the pre-cut interlining pieces.

13. **Piping the shoulder seams**. Cut bias strips as before, but 1¾ in / 45 mm wide. Join to make up 1½ yd / 1.35 m. Align the raw edges of the bias strips and that of the sleeve armhole, so that the finished piping is ¼ in / 6 mm wide, as before.

14. Join the jacket and the sleeve around the armhole, matching dots, single and double notches respectively. Pin and machine-stitch, stopping at the small dot marked at each end of the sleeve armhole. Repeat for 2nd sleeve. Trim off ½ in / 15 mm from both wrists.

15. **Cuffs**. For each, cut and piece 8 strips 1¼ x 17½ in / 3.2 x 44.5 cm in the following sequence: striped, black, pale grey, bronze, black, pale grey, mid-grey and striped. Press. Using the chevron pattern from a section of the front lapel pattern, cord quilt both cuffs as in paragraph 7. Attach the cuffs to the sleeves, right sides facing.

16. To complete the side seams of the garment, match underarm dots. Pin the front and the back of the jacket, then the sleeve

seams, ensuring that the stripes on the cuffs align accurately. The ends of the armhole piping should be hidden in the seam allowance. Trim back excess wadding / batting and interlining to reduce bulk in the seams. Turn back the cuffs inside the sleeve and tack / baste along the folded edge to hold in position.

17. **Pockets**. For each, cut 2 strips of black and 1 strip of pale grey silk, 2 x 25 in / 5 x 64 cm. With a set square, mark and cut 4 right-angled triangles (see **diagram 5.**). Join 2 triangles along their shorter sides. Repeat, matching the seams to make a square. Press all seams to 1 side. Repeat for 2nd pocket. Cut 2 squares of muslin to the same size. Pin to the back of the pocket. Machine-stitch parallel lines *around* the square, starting along the seam lines between the coloured strips. Using the width of the machine foot as a guide, stitch channels ¼ in / 6 mm apart as with the chevron pattern on the lapels. Cord quilt as before, leaving the outer channel unthreaded.

18. The pockets are piped on 3 sides, the open side showing a glimpse of red lining. Prepare 2 yd / 1.80 m of bias strips, 1½ in / 38 mm wide. Measure 1 side of the pocket. Cut 3 strips of bias to that length. Turn in ¼ in / 38 mm at both ends. Pin on to 1 side of the pocket (right side up) and with the folded edge of the piping inwards. Position the corners as shown on **diagram 6.** on the opposite page and machine-stitch. Insert quilting wool in the final channel which you had left empty. Push the raw edges of the pocket and the piping towards the wrong side of the pocket and fix with a row of herringbone stitch. Repeat for 2nd pocket.

19. **Lining the pockets**. Cut 2 10¾ in / 27.5 cm squares out of the lining fabric. Pin, right sides together, to the top of the pocket. Machine-stitch. Smooth over the back of the pocket. Turn the raw edges of the lining under and slip-stitch over the piping stitching line. Repeat for 2nd pocket. Try on the jacket and position the pockets at a comfortable height. Top-stitch 'in the hollow' as you did for the lapels (see paragraph 9 above).

Northern Star Quilters' Guild, Ltd
P.O. Box 232 Somers, N.Y. 10589

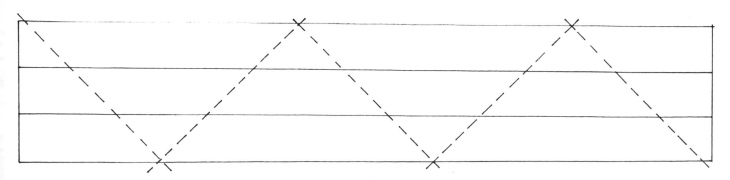

Diagram 5. *For each pocket, machine-stitch 2 black strips with a pale grey one in the middle, cut to the dimensions given in the text. With a set square, trace 4 right-angled triangles as shown above. This diagram is not to scale.*

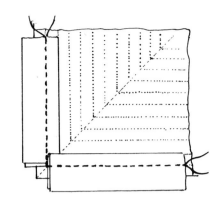

20. **Lining the jacket**. Use the paper pattern to cut the lining, but adding to the measurements as follows, for ease of movement and extra turnings. *To the fronts* add: 1 in / 25 mm to inner front edges and ½ in / 15 mm to the side seams; 2 in / 5 cm to neck curve as it rises from the shoulder seam; and 2 in / 5 cm to the length of the jacket. *To the back* side seams add ½ in / 13 mm; 1½ in / 38 mm to neck edge; 1½ in / 38 mm to the length. Shorten sleeves at the broken line, as marked on pattern. Transfer notches and dots as usual. Tack / baste to mark the centre of the back.

21. Attach the fronts to the back of the lining, along the shoulder seam. Stop where the shoulder seam rises to the neck. Stitch the sleeves to the armholes, then the sleeve side seams and the side seams of the jacket lining. Fit *over* the jacket, right sides together, and check the fit of the shoulder / neck line which should correspond with the shape of the jacket shoulder / lapel. Pin the remainder of the lining shoulder / neck seams and remove lining from jacket. Complete the curved shoulder / neck seams, clipping the seam edges. Press as you go, opening the seams out flat.

22. Fit the lining inside the jacket, wrong sides together, and pin at strategic points to hold in position. At the centre top sleeve and shoulder seam junction, work several stitches on the spot to hold this point securely. Pin along shoulder seams. Pin and tack / baste the centre back lines together. Repeat for the side seams.

23. Hang up the garment so that the lining hangs naturally. Turn the inside front edges under and pin to the inside front edges of the jacket and to the back lapel, covering the inside of the garment, flush up to the piping. Trim off any excess fabric and ensure that the lining does not tug. Slip-stitch the lining, leaving a 6 in / 15 cm gap around the position of the frog fastening. With the sleeves turned inside out, so that the lining is facing, turn under the edge of the lining to cover the raw edge of each cuff which was left folded back and tacked / basted into position (see paragraph 16).

24. **The hem of the garment**. Adjust the hemline of the jacket to the length required. Mark the fold of the hem with a line of tacking / basting. Trim back excess wadding and interlining to the fold line. Re-pin the hem. Attach with a row of herringbone stitch. Trim the length of the lining to 1 in / 25 mm below the edge of the jacket. Turn 1¼ in / 32 mm at the base of the lining. Pin it to the bottom of the jacket. Hang the jacket to check that the lining does not sag or pull. Slip-stitch.

25. Attach the frog fastening. Slip-stitch the open section of the lining. To finish off the garment, work a small decorative stitch, just inside the edges of the garment, around the front and back lapels, using coton perlé and stitching into the back of the lapels, ensuring that it does not show on the right side of the jacket. This will hold the lining in place.

Diagram 6. *Detail of the pocket corner. The piping is applied on the right side of the corded pocket square. The ends of the piping are turned under ¼ in / 6 mm at the corners.*

Below. *The finished pocket with the striped piping. The red silk lining peeps out slightly at the top of the pocket.*

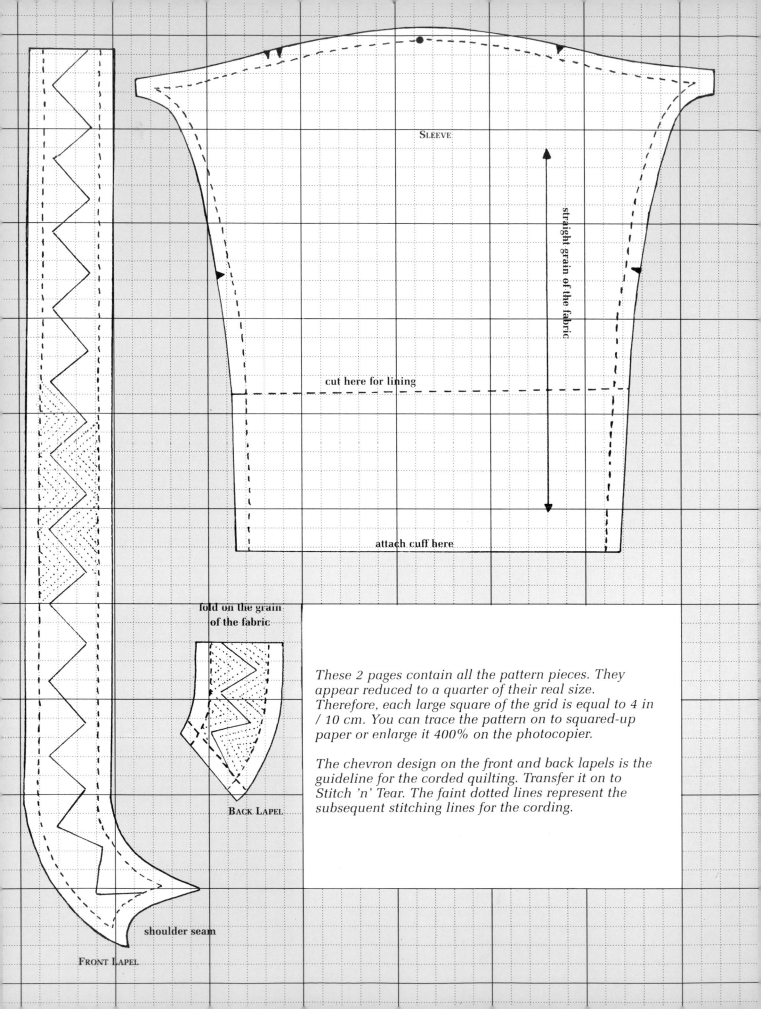

SLEEVE

straight grain of the fabric

cut here for lining

attach cuff here

fold on the grain
of the fabric

BACK LAPEL

shoulder seam

FRONT LAPEL

*These 2 pages contain all the pattern pieces. They
appear reduced to a quarter of their real size.
Therefore, each large square of the grid is equal to 4 in
/ 10 cm. You can trace the pattern on to squared-up
paper or enlarge it 400% on the photocopier.*

*The chevron design on the front and back lapels is the
guideline for the corded quilting. Transfer it on to
Stitch 'n' Tear. The faint dotted lines represent the
subsequent stitching lines for the cording.*

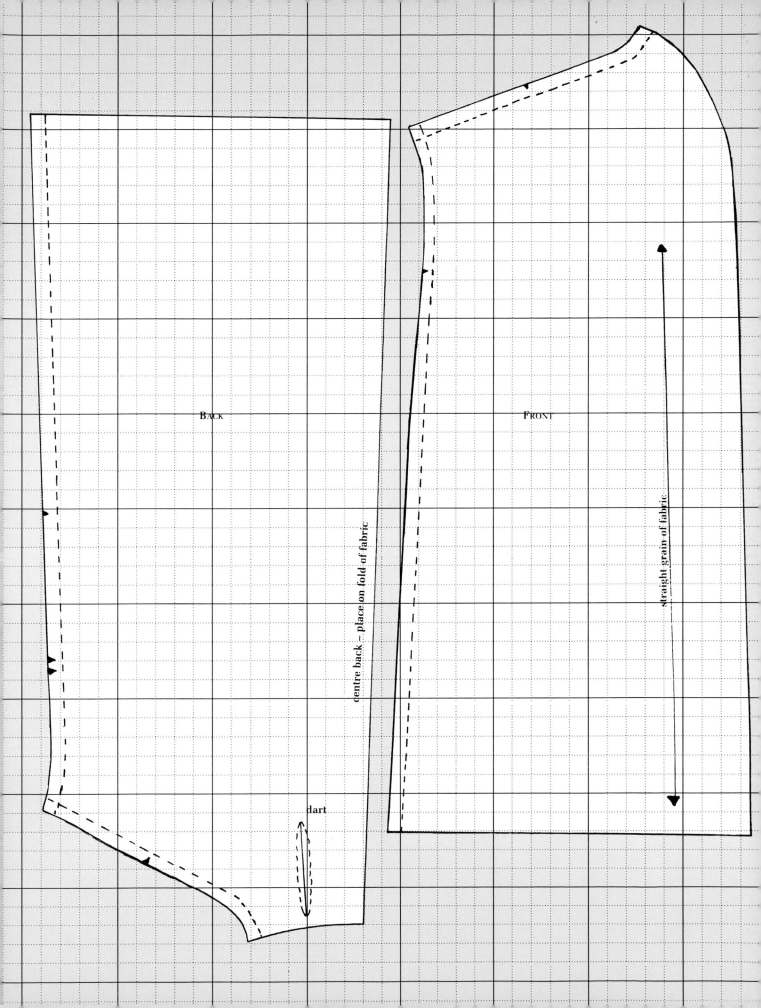

BACK

FRONT

centre back – place on fold of fabric

straight grain of fabric

dart

CREAM-COLOURED WALLHANGING

Gilly Wraight

SHOPPING LIST

3 yd / 2.70 m of unbleached calico,
40 in / 102 cm wide
5 18 in / 45 cm squares of toning cotton
fabrics
1 oblong 28 x 40 in / 75 x 102 cm of
lightweight wadding / batting
4 large buttons (horn) *and* 1 even larger
(a sliver of ammonite was used here)
wooden and dull metallic beads in an
assortment of shapes and sizes
écru machine-sewing thread *and* strong
quilting thread, *also* in a contrasting
colour
10 small, non-rusting curtain rings

I have always been fascinated by the inventiveness displayed in early American quilts. The makers, who were often poor homesteaders, used up old clothes and flour sacking and out of these humble, dull-coloured materials they produced heirlooms. I used unbleached calico for this piece, together with traditionally patterned cotton fabrics – a tiny floral design and checks – and combined them with bold shapes and textures to give the hanging a modern feel.

1. The hanging is made up of 5 blocks, mostly crazy patchwork. (Refer to photographs opposite and to the pattern on page 43.) Enlarge the pattern on page 43, as instructed. The thick lines show the outlines of the 5 blocks. The pieces within each block are numbered to show the working order. Cut out the individual templates within each block. Out of the calico, on the straight grain of the fabric, cut 1 oblong 28 x 40 in / 71 x 100 cm. This will form the back of the hanging. Also cut a piece 22 x 18 in / 56 x 45 cm for the foundation fabric of block E. Cut 2 strips 28 x 4 in / 71 x 10 cm; then 2 39 x 4 in / 99 x 10 cm. These will form the border of the hanging. On the bias, cut 2 strips 30 x 2 in / 76 x 5 cm, then 2 strips 41 x 2 in / 104 x 5 cm – they will be used to bind the edges of the hanging. On the straight grain of the fabric, cut 4 oblongs 11 x 9 in / 28 x 23 cm – the foundation fabric for blocks A., B., C. and D.

2. **Block E.** The background of this block is made up of shapes applied by machine, according to the crazy patchwork method. The flower is made of quill patchwork and will be appliqued at a later stage. Using the numbered templates for that block, cut the relevant 13 shapes out of calico and the remaining 4 out of the specified fabrics. Add ¼ in / 6 mm all round for the seams. Number the pieces on the right side of the cloth, using tailor's chalk. Place the paper templates over the right side of the foundation material for block E. and trace around them (no seam allowance here) with a sharp, hard pencil.

3. Refer to the crazy patchwork method on page 113 and, starting with 1., apply each shape in turn until the foundation fabric is covered. Do not worry too much about the centre of the block, where the lines converge – it will be covered by the flower. Make up **Block B.** in the same way.

4. **Block A.** Cut the shapes as instructed above, except for No. 1., which is made of ruched calico. Cut a piece of fabric,

Above. *The wallhanging was made up to hang horizontally, but it could just as well be hung the other way round. Its finished measurements are 26 x 37½ in / 66 x 95 cm.*

Left. *A detail from Block C. The square of double ruching has been heavily encrusted with tiny beads.*

Folding and making quills. Normally, you should slip-stitch them at the back. It was unnecessary here as they are firmly held together by the lines of machine-stitching which also fix them to the wallhanging.

Making a length of 'ribbon'.

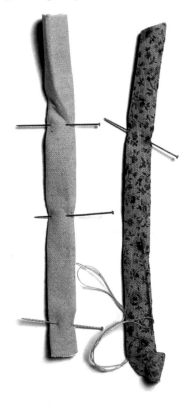

about twice the length of the template and about 2 in / 5 cm wider. Set the sewing-machine stitch to its longest available length and run a line of gathers along the 2 long dimensions of the fabric piece. Pull the threads until the piece is just over the size of the original template. Apply it to the foundation material as if it were a normal piece of flat fabric. Attach the other shapes in order.

5. **Block C.** Shape 1. is made of double ruching. Cut a piece 10 in / 26 cm square. Set the machine to its longest available stitch and run lines of gathers across the width and length of the fabric, approximately 1 in / 25 mm apart. Leave long threads at the end of each row to gather the fabric. Pull these threads carefully, in both directions, until the patch is just a little larger than the template. Complete the block. **Block D**. The focal point of this block is a square of log cabin patchwork (see page 117), framed by crazy patchwork patches, applied as before.

6. **The quill patchwork flower**. This provides a dramatic focal point to block E. Out of the calico, cut 35 strips 5 x 4 in / 13 x 10 cm. Fold to make quills (see left above and refer to the endpapers of this book, which show a close-up of the flower motif). Mark the centre of block E. Draw a circle about 2 in / 5 cm across and start laying the quills, overlapping them slightly at the centre. Cut them shorter as you get to the second layer. Finish off with 3 or 4 very short quills, making sure that the button, or whatever will form the centre of the flower, covers the raw edges. Tack / baste the quills into position. I have also used lengths of 'ribbon', made up of narrow strips of calico and printed fabric. Turn in the raw edges, fold in half and press to form a flat ribbon. Slip-stitch the edges. Tuck under the quills. Slip-stitch or machine-top-stitch into position. Run lines of top-stitching over the quills, using contrasting thread (refer to endpaper picture). Cut small rectangles of the check fabric, wrap them around the smaller pieces of wadding / batting and applique them to the left-hand side of block E. Attach 3 short quills to block B. Fix the buttons. Scatter beads over the work as desired. Join the 4 blocks together, then join to block E. Square off the panel to a finished size of 20½ x 32 in / 52 x 81 cm.

7. **The border** Attach the strips (refer to para 6 on page 58). Press. The border should be 3¼ in / 8 cm wide. Trim excess cloth. Lay the backing of the hanging on the table, then the wadding / batting, and place the front of the hanging, right side up, over it. Tack / baste. Trim off excess fabric. Hand-quilt close to the seams around the blocks. Machine-stitch the bias edging along the 2 short dimensions of the hanging, allowing for ⅝ in / 15 mm seam allowance. Fold over the raw edge of the hanging. Turn the raw edge of the strip under and hand-hem over the line of machine stitches. Repeat for the 2 long dimensions. Attach the curtain rings at regular intervals below the top edge of the back of the hanging so that they do not show when it hangs on the wall.

Below. The pattern for the wallhanging. The thick lines show the outlines of the 5 blocks. The pattern has been reduced to a quarter of its real size. Therefore enlarge each block on the photocopier 400%. The numbers refer to the working order within each block.

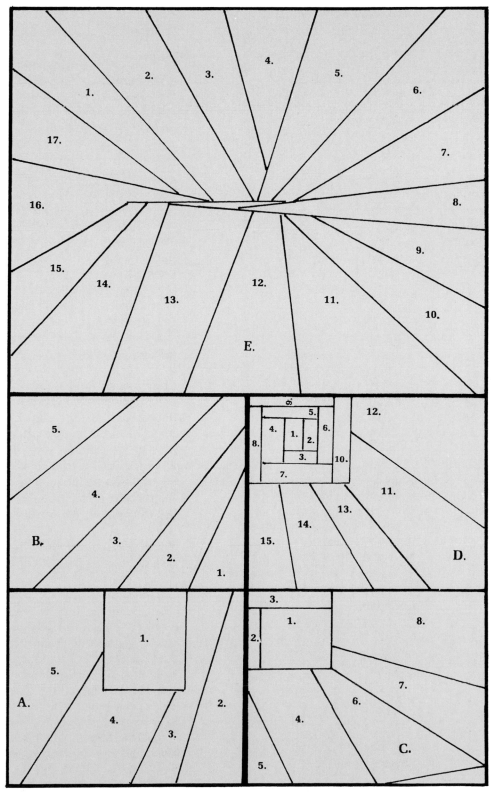

BLOCK E
2. = floral fabric
6. and 15. = check fabric
9. = plain dark fabric

BLOCK B
1. = floral fabric
4. = check fabric

BLOCK A
1. = single ruching
5. = floral fabric

BLOCK C
1. = double ruching
4. = single ruching
5. = floral fabric

BLOCK D
1.–10. = log cabin patch
11. = ruching

43

CRAZY PATCHWORK WALLHANGING

Gisela Thwaites

This small wallhanging is embellished with beads, sequins and shishas, couched threads and ribbons, as usual. I also used scraps of a finely pleated Indian stretch rayon fabric. It does not fray and can be manipulated into knots and appliqued over the work.

1. Refer to instructions for crazy patchwork on page 113. Use small patches and balance the light and dark tones carefully until the foundation material is entirely covered.

2. Refer to the paragraph headed **General principles** on page 20 and to the picture of the hanging opposite. The circular patch next to the blue 'scrunch' was worked 'in the hand', using sequins, beads and a few embroidery stitches; it was appliqued by hand over the patchwork background. The 'scrunches' are held in place with a few slip stitches. I traced the outline of the red heart over the patchwork patch and fixed several rows of tiny glass beads over it. Add a few shishas (refer to instructions on page 94).

3. **Finishing off the patchwork panel.** Lay the piece of embellished patchwork over the oblong of wadding / batting. Tack / baste together. Square off piece so that it measures 20 x 10 in / 50 x 25 cm. Out of the dark-coloured silk, cut 2 strips 36 x 2½ in / 90 x 6.5 cm. Join them to make a continuous one. Machine-stitch, right sides together, ⅝ in / 15 mm from the edges of the panel, mitring corners and finishing off, as instructed on page 122. (We are not using a double strip here, but the method for mitring the corners remains the same.)

4. **Background panel and loops.** Place the remaining dark silk face down over the table. Position the piece of pelmet-weight interlining over it. The silk should be 5 in / 13 cm longer than the interlining at the bottom and 3 in / 80 mm taller and larger along the other dimensions (see sketch). Out of the offcuts, cut 5 strips 5½ x 2¾ in / 14 x 70 mm. Machine-stitch lengthwise, ¼ in / 6 mm away from the edge, to form a tube. Turn right side out. Position the seam at the centre of the loop and press flat. Fold the excess fabric over the top of the interlining panel. Tack / baste. Attach the loops with a few stitches. Fold the sides over, then the excess fabric at the bottom, mitring corners. Pin. Work a herringbone stitch along the raw edges of the fabric (they will be hidden by the patchwork panel). Position patchwork over base of loops and slip-stitch into position. Attach bottom corners of patchwork panel to background with a few stitches.

The construction of the background panel. The hashed area represents the interlining. The patchwork panel is then slip-stitched over the base of the loops, hiding the raw edges.

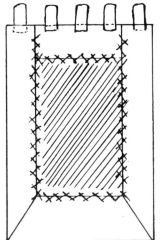

CUSHIONS &
MATCHING BOLSTER

✿

Jill Essery

Flowing graceful fish shapes have been stencilled and quilted as a pair of cushions and a bolster. By re-arranging their position, a new design has been achieved on each object. Make 1 or all 3 to add a fresh, elegant look to your bedroom or living room.

1. For each cushion cut 1 19 in / 48 cm square of white habutai. For the bolster cut 1 oblong 21 x 9¾ in / 53.5 x 25 cm of white habutai. Cut wadding / batting and muslin to the same sizes. Put aside.

2. Enlarge the fish and wave motifs on page 50, as instructed. Make card or acetate stencils. For the square cushions, lightly mark the centre lines by folding the fabric in half, both ways, and finger-pressing. On pages 49-50 you will see sketches showing the positioning of the fish and the wave patterns within each piece (the wave design was not used on the 1st cushion). These sketches can be enlarged if you need an extra guide. Remember that they are intended as a guide only. The charm of stencilling is its spontaneity and you can find your own arrangement for the shapes. The quilting lines follow the outlines of the fish and waves. Study the sketches and you'll see that in my versions, the fish motifs form concentric circles in the 1st cushion and flow radially from the centre in the 2nd, with the wave pattern forming a border near the edge of the cushion. The bolster is worked along diagonal lines which spiral around it.

3. **Painting the fabric.** Cover the table with plastic sheeting and several sheets of absorbent paper. Hold the silk down with masking tape. Prepare a *weak* solution of blue paint. Using the sprayer (practise on a scrap of silk first), spray lightly over some areas of the silk, so that it is shaded randomly. Allow to dry (use a hair-dryer to speed up the process if you like). Prepare a range of iridescent blue, green and turquoise paints in little dishes. Have clean water, paper towels and some scraps of fabric to try out the strength of the colours and the consistency of the paint at the ready. Position the stencils, starting from the centre of the piece of fabric. Apply paint sparingly to the stencilling brush or sponge. Use a dabbing motion to apply the paint to the fabric to give a stippled effect. If you have too much paint on the brush or if the silk becomes sodden, the colour will bleed under the stencil ends or you may have heavy splodges of colour. As the shapes often overlap and the stencil cards are used on both sides, depending on the direction and curve of the fish,

---

SHOPPING LIST

⅔ yd / 60 cm of white silk habutai, 36 in / 90 cm wide for the front of each cushion

¾ yd / 70 cm of white silk habutai, 36 in / 90 cm wide for the bolster

½ yd / 45 cm of turquoise or green silk (dupion or Thai silk) for the back of 1 cushion, 36 in / 90 cm wide (the width of the fabric is sufficient to back the 2nd cushion too)

¼ yd / 25 cm of blue silk dupion for the ends of the bolster

scraps of 4 or 5 different silks, ranging from turquoise to green, for the applique

½ yd / 45 cm green silk for piping

2 yd / 1.80 m of butter muslin

2 yd / 1.80 m of medium-weight polyester wadding / batting

¼ yd / 25 cm lightweight iron-on interfacing

1 small piece of pelmet-weight Vilene

machine-embroidery thread (metallic silver, metallic turquoise, pale variegated ivory / blue)

5½ yd / 5 m piping cord No. 4

2 16 in / 40 cm square cushion pads

1 18 in / 45 cm long, 6¾ in / 17 cm in diameter bolster pad

freezer paper

permanent fabric paints – a range of iridescent colours in blue, turquoise and green

card or acetate for templates and stencil

stencil brushes or sponge

hand-spray bottle (the type used for houseplants is perfect)

plastic sheeting and absorbent paper to protect the work surface

small dishes for the paint, jars for clean water, paper towels

masking tape

Both cushions measure 15½ / 40 cm square. The bolster is 18 in / 46 cm long with a diameter of 7 in / 18 cm.

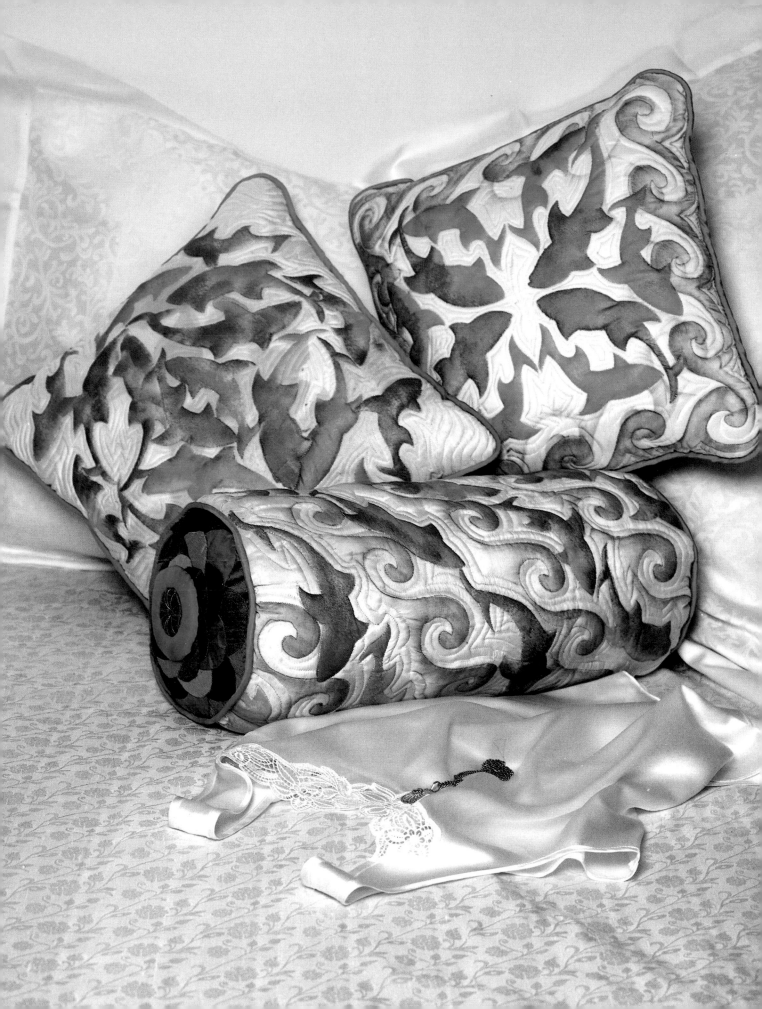

you must avoid smudging wet paint where it is not wanted. Allow these areas to dry before working over them again (the hair-dryer is useful). Once all the stencilling is done, fix according to the manufacturer's instructions.

4. **Quilting the work**. Place the piece of muslin on the table, then the wadding / batting, with the stencilled silk, right side up, on top. Tack / baste. (Refer to general instructions on page 121.) Machine-quilt the outlines of the stencilled shapes, using iridescent turquoise machine-embroidery thread on top and ordinary sewing thread in the bobbin. NOTE: it is important to work from the centre outwards, and to proceed evenly in all directions, even to the point of working 1 side of a shape only. Leave loose tails of thread and start again from the original point rather than going all the way round the shape in a continuous line. This is to avoid fabric getting trapped in an enclosed area and causing unsightly puckers. Where shapes overlap, decide which is uppermost, and stop and start accordingly. Stitch slowly, lifting the foot with the needle in the fabric. Smooth the fabric, easing the fullness with your hand, and stitch further. You may find a darning foot useful. When all the shapes are outlined pull all the thread ends to the back, knot and trim to ½ in / 15 mm. Change the top thread to a pale variegated or silver embroidery thread. Contour-quilt around and between the main shapes, using the width of the machine foot to space the quilting lines evenly (study the colour details opposite). Accentuate angles, wherever necessary, to emphasize the flowing wave and fish shapes. Work from the centre as before. The quilting should not extend beyond ½ in / 15 mm of the edge of the work. When finished, neaten all the hanging threads, as before.

5. Measure the quilted front of each cushion. Trim off excess fabric to leave a 17 in / 43 cm square (which includes a ⅝ in / 15 mm seam allowance all round).

6. **Piping and assembling a cushion**. Refer to instructions on piping on page 124. Out of the chosen silk fabric, cut bias strips 2¼ in / 5.7 cm wide. Join to make a continuous length of 30 in / 76 cm. Use piping cord No. 4 and fit a zipper foot on the sewing machine to stitch close to the cord. If your machine has an adjustable needle position, set this appropriately too. Place the work right side up and pin the piping all round the cushion, starting in the middle of 1 side, and with the folded edge of the piping pointing towards the centre of the work. Curve gently around the corners, rather than making sharply angled turns. Clip the raw edges of the piping to ease round. Unpick 1 in / 2.5 cm of the machine stitches at one end. Cut off the excess cord so that the 2 ends butt against each other. Fold the unpicked end of the fabric under and wrap it over the other cut end to encase it neatly.

7. **The back of the cushion**. Out of the chosen silk fabric, cut a 17 in / 43 cm square. Pin to the front of the cushion, right

sides together, and machine-stitch all round, leaving a 9 in / 23 cm gap. Turn the case right side out. Insert the pad. Slip-stitch the opening. Both cushions are made up in exactly the same way.

8. **The bolster**. Wrap the stencilled and quilted top around the bolster pad to obtain an accurate measurement for the case. Trim off excess fabric, allowing 1 in / 2.5 cm all round for seam allowances. Machine-stitch the side seam, leaving a 9 in / 23 cm gap. Insert the pad and pin the opening shut. Measure the diameter of the bolster (including the thickness of the quilted case). Add 1 in / 2.5 cm for the seam allowance. Use a compass to draw a circle of card to that total diameter. Cut out. Use as a template to cut 4 circles out of the chosen silk, 2 out of iron-on interlining.

9. **The appliqued ends of the bolster**. Enlarge **template 1.** on page 50. Use it to trace the shapes on to the *shiny* side of a piece of freezer paper. Follow the method outlined in paragraphs 3. and 4. of page 75-76. In this case, start with the outer shapes, overlapping the next rows like fish scales and appliqueing them over 1 circle of the silk as you go. When you have finished, make tiny slits at the back of the motif to extricate the paper shapes.

10. The ends of the bolster have a sort of soft button in the centre. Enlarge **template 2.** and use its centre section to cut a circle of pelmet-weight Vilene and 1 of wadding / batting. Use the whole template to cut a circle of green silk. Run a row of gathers, just inside the outside edge of the silk circle. Place the wadding / batting disc over the Vilene, then the silk, pulling the gathering thread and securing it at the back to produce a soft padded shape. Use **template 3.** to make a smaller button in exactly the same way. After pulling the gathering thread, decorate this smaller circle with long radial stitches of fine metallic thread, working from near the centre point, right over the edge and back towards the centre. Pull the thread lightly to produce a slight indentation in the padding. Attach the circles to each other and fix them firmly at the centre of the applique. Take 1 of the 3 remaining circles of silk cut in paragraph 8. Attach 1 circle of iron-on interlining to it. Tack / baste to the appliqued circle, wrong sides together (the interlining will be between the 2 layers of silk). Prepare 27 in / 68 cm of piping, as before. Apply to the edge of the circle. Repeat for the other end of the bolster.

11. With the bolster pad inside the case, pin 1 end of the bolster in position as if it were a lid. Position the pins very close to each other, easing the fullness as you go. This is an unconventional method but it is a lot easier than trying to attach the circular end around the circumference of the tube by machine, as the quilting gets in the way. To avoid pinning and stitching into the pad, insert a piece of acetate under the seam area. It is flexible enough to go round the curve but the needle will not go through it. Slip-stitch all round. Repeat for the other end. Slip-stitch the side opening.

Opposite. *Details from the cushions.*

Above. *Sketches showing the arrangement of the stencilled motifs of the 2 cushions. A sketch of the bolster appears at the bottom of page 50. They are not to scale, but you may find it helpful to enlarge them as a guide.*

Below. *This sketch shows how the 2 soft 'buttons' (see paragraph 10.) overlap each other. The radial stitches produce indentations.*

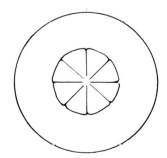

Enlarge all the shapes under yellow tint 200%.

a., b., c. and **d.** are the stencil motifs. Cut out of firm card or acetate.
Hollow out the fish shapes.

Template 1. is used for the appliqued ends of the bolster.
The dotted line is the cutting line. Sketch **1a.** shows how the
shapes overlap like scales. Use as a guide to produce the
applique motif. Work in the numbered sequence and
continue until the shape is complete. **Template 2.**
Use the entire circle to cut the silk to cover
the large 'button' and the inner circle to
cut the interlining. **Template 3.**
is used to produce the smaller
'button'. The sketch, bottom left,
shows the arrangement of the
motifs on the bolster.

STENCILLED & APPLIQUED EVENING JACKET

❧

Christine Donaldson

This exquisite and timeless jacket will team up happily with the perennial 'little black dress' or with trousers. The fan motif is made out of crazy patchwork and of American seamed patchwork, both techniques worked on the machine (see pages 113 and 114 for step-by-step instructions). The fans are appliqued with machine satin stitch, using contrasting and metallic threads. A simple stencilled fan shape forms a border which echoes the appliqued motifs. The jacket itself is easy to cut out and sew.

Seam allowances on the jacket are ⅝ in / 15 mm
Seam allowances on the patchwork are ¼ in / 6 mm

1. Using the pattern shown on pages 54-55, enlarge the pieces by 400% using a photocopier or trace on to squared-up dress-making paper. Cut the 5 pieces out of your main fabric and repeat for the lining. If the jacket fabric is loosely woven, like the Jarpur silk we have used, stay-stitch around each piece, approximately ⅛ in / 3 mm from the edge, to prevent fraying.

2. Using the template on the opposite page, trace off the fan stencil and transfer to the oiled manilla paper or acetate. Cut out with a sharp knife.

3. Using the prepared stencil with a brush or the small sponge piece (I prefer the sponge) and fabric paint, make a test on an offcut from the jacket fabric. Don't use too much paint at first – it is easy to add if you haven't used enough, but much more difficult to remove excess paint! The beauty of stencilling is that the design will appear with varying intensity of colour, so don't try to make every motif a perfect copy of its neighbour. Using a fade-out fabric marker or a line of tacking / basting stitches, mark the seam line ⅝ in / 15 mm away from the edge. This will ensure that the stencilled shapes fall in the right places.

Previous page. Emma *wearing the jacket.*

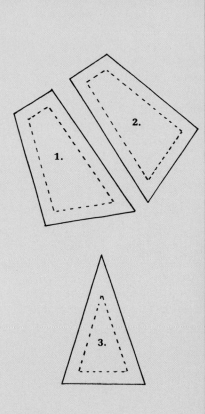

Enlarge all the shapes on this page 200% as they have been reproduced exactly half size.

Above. The 3 American patchwork templates. For one fan, cut each shape 3 times. The photographic detail shows one American patchwork fan on the left and, on the right, one made of crazy patchwork.

Right. The crazy patchwork template. The dotted lines indicate the lines of satin stitch which represent the ribs of the fan.

Left. The stencil. Cut out the inner pattern carefully, using a sharp knife.

The pattern is reproduced exactly quarter size. Each large square is equal to 4 in / 10 cm. You can trace it and have the pattern enlarged or transfer it to squared-up pattern paper.

4. Once you are happy with your stencilling skills, apply 3 motifs on the lower part of both jacket fronts; 1 each on top, near the neck line (see photograph). These 2 will be partly overlapped by the appliqued motifs. Paint 3 more on the lower part of the back of the jacket. Allow the paint to dry and fix the colour according to the manufacturer's instructions.

5. Make up the jacket, joining the centre back seam, then the shoulder and side seams. Press all seams open.

6. Join the underarm seams in the sleeves and press open. Matching the underarm seams of the sleeves with the side seams of the jacket, right sides together, set in each sleeve, easing to fit. Trim and clip seams. Press.

7. Using the fan template on page 53 and the instructions for machine applique on page 120, make up 3 'crazy' fans, using the lightweight interfacing as the base.

8. Using the 3 templates on page 53 and the instructions for American seamed patchwork on page 114, make up 6 patchwork fans. Press carefully, then cut off the ¼ in / 6 mm seam allowance all around the completed fans.

front of sleeve

straight grain of fabric

SLEEVE
cut 2 of main fabric
and 2 of lining

9. Position the 'crazy' and the patchwork fans to your satisfaction. Pin and tack / baste into place. Satin-stitch around the motifs. Press.

10. Make up the jacket lining in 2 halves, i.e. do not join the centre back seam.

11. With right sides together, pin and tack / baste both sides of the lining to their corresponding sides of the jacket at the lower edge of the sleeves (points). Stitch, then trim off excess fabric from the points, snipping to the stitching line at the inner angles. Press.

12. Right sides together, join the centre back of the lining. Machine-stitch lining to jacket, along the front edges and around the neck. Trim seams and clip into angles of neck detail. Trim seams and clip into angles. Turn inside out. Press.

13. Turn a narrow hem and hand-stitch around the lower edge of the jacket. Repeat for the lining, but making the hem slightly deeper to ensure that it does not hang below the jacket. Press.

14. Cut a piece of card 1¾ in / 45 mm deep. Following instructions on page 124, make 9 small tassels. Add a bead to the top of each. Sew firmly to 3 points on each sleeve and to 3 of the fans on the jacket front and back.

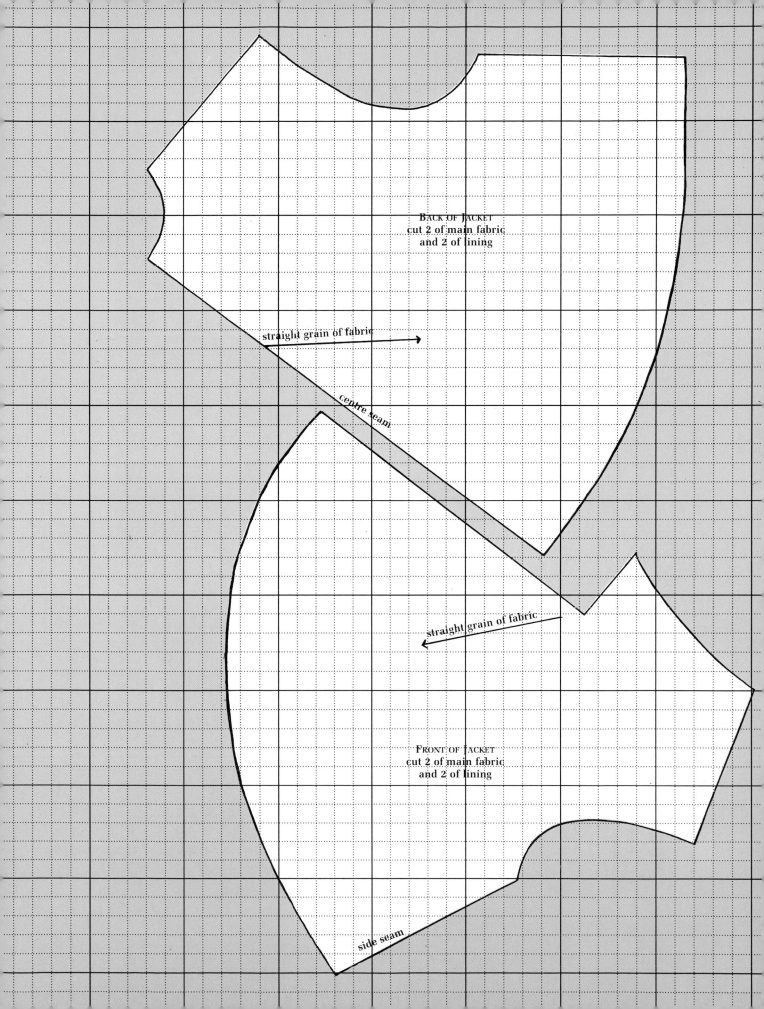

BACK OF JACKET
cut 2 of main fabric
and 2 of lining

straight grain of fabric

centre seam

straight grain of fabric

FRONT OF JACKET
cut 2 of main fabric
and 2 of lining

side seam

CRETAN FLOOR CUSHION

Gilly Wraight

This American pieced patchwork floor cushion was inspired by the rich geometric or floral counted-thread embroidery practised on Crete. The traditional colours for the embroidery are a rich red and black. This cushion will throw a splash of colour in any room.

1. Out of the red cotton material, cut 2 bands 16½ x 6 in / 42 x 15 cm and 2 24¾ x 6 in / 63 x 15 cm. These will eventually form the border around the cushion. Out of the black cotton fabric cut a piece 25½ in / 65 cm square. This will form the back of the cushion.

2. Copy the 2 triangular and the square templates on page 59 and make a cardboard master for each. Make a tracing of the flower motif.

3. Out of the red fabric, cut 8 squares and 16 *small* triangles, using the prepared templates. Out of the black fabric, cut 8 squares and 8 *large* triangles. Cut a piece of even-weave linen, large enough to contain 4 times the square template, allowing for 1 in / 25 mm all round. Trace round the square template lightly with a sharp hard pencil, then transfer the sewing lines and the motif. Do not cut out the 4 individual squares yet, or the linen will fray while you work the embroidery. Apply iron-on interlining to the back of the remaining linen and use the templates to cut 16 *small* and 8 *large* triangles out of it.

4. You will see that 2 of the squares have a red embroidered flower, with the linen background left bare. The other 2 have a red embroidered background with the linen left bare inside the flower. In both cases, the embroidery is cross stitch, worked over 2 threads of the linen. The centres of the flowers are also in cross stitch. Outline the flowers in back stitch. With a hot iron, fix a piece of iron-on interlining at the back of the embroidered squares and cut them out.

5. **American seamed patchwork panel.** Refer to the general instructions on page 114. The diagram on page 58 shows the arrangement of the shapes and colours within the patchwork panel. Start by joining 2 small triangles to form a large one. Join this to a large triangle to make a square. Join the resulting square to another. Join the 2 squares to a 3rd one. Make up the next 2 rows of squares. Join the completed 3 rows to each other to make a 9-patch square. Repeat 3 times. Join the 4 resulting squares to each other. Press.

Northern Star Quilters' Guild Ltd
P.O. Box 232 Somers, N.Y. 10589

Opposite. *The finished cushion measures 23½ in / 60 cm square.*

This diagram shows the arrangement of shapes and colours within the patchwork panel.

6. **The cushion border**. When the patchwork is completed, take one of the smaller oblongs of red fabric, which you cut in 1. above, and lay it right sides together over one side of the patchwork panel. Pin and machine-stitch, ¼ in / 6 mm from the edge. Attach the 2nd short oblong to the opposite side of the patchwork panel. Pin and machine-stitch 1 of the longer border pieces on to the 3rd side of the cushion and repeat for the 4th. Press. The width of the border should be 5 in / 13 cm all round, inclusive of a ⅝ in / 15 mm seam allowance. Trim off if necessary.

7. **Assembling the cushion**. Lay the piece of calico flat on the table. Place the cushion front, face up, over it. Cut the calico to the same size. Tack / baste together. Top-stitch along the edge of the patchwork panel to fix the top of the cushion to the calico lining. This will reinforce the patchwork and prevent the seams from splitting with use. Lay the square of black cotton fabric over the table. Lay the cushion front, face down, over it. Trim excess black fabric. Pin and machine-stitch, leaving a 14 in / 36 cm gap for turning the work inside out. Insert the pad. Slip-stitch the opening.

black

red

écru

58

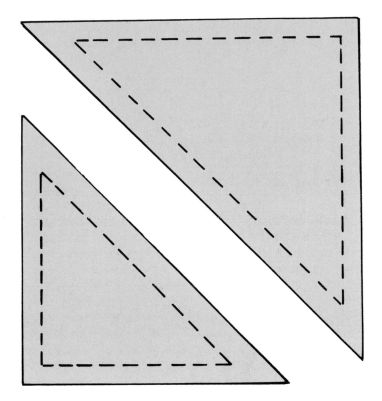

These 3 templates are shown lifesize.

This detail shows 1 of the 9-patch squares. The background of the flower is embroidered in cross stitch and the flower itself is kept as a negative shape.

BUTTERFLY KIMONO

Christine Donaldson

Below. *Enlarge the 4 butterflies 200%.*

Opposite page. *The finished kimono.*

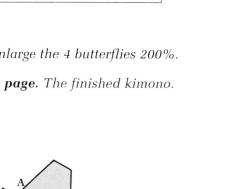

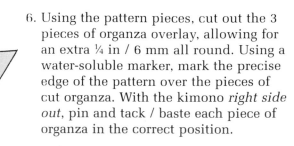

Brilliantly coloured butterflies flutter across a kimono-shaped plain silk negligee. This one was bought ready-made but it can easily be cut at home. This decorative technique can be used on a variety of garments. The bright colours of the silk butterflies are muted by an organza overlay. This shadow quilting makes use of contemporary sewing aids such as tear-off backing material and is outlined with machine-stitching and machine-satin stitch, made with a lovely shade of machine-embroidery thread.

1. Enlarge the butterfly shapes below and make cardboard templates. Enlarge the organza overlay pieces shown on page 62 and make paper patterns.

2. Refer to the instructions for machine applique on page 120. Using the paper-backed fusible web and the prepared templates, mark and cut out 5 'A' type butterflies, 3 of 'B' type, 3 of 'C' and 3 of 'D'.

3. To help you position the butterflies, pin the organza overlay patterns over the back and front of the kimono and run a line of tacking / basting around them, to mark the edge of the pattern. Do not stitch through the pattern paper. Position 9 butterflies within the marked area at the back of the kimono, 4 on the front right-hand side and one on the left front (make sure it will show when the kimono is worn).

4. Still referring to the machine-applique instructions on page 120, iron the butterfly shapes into position. Using the overlay pattern, cut 3 pieces out of the tear-off backing material, allowing for an extra ¼ in / 6 mm all around the 3 shapes.

5. With the kimono *wrong side out*, place each relevant piece of tear-off backing material over the area outlined with tacking / basting. Pin and tack / baste tear-off material in position, ensuring that the fabric of the kimono is kept absolutely flat.

6. Using the pattern pieces, cut out the 3 pieces of organza overlay, allowing for an extra ¼ in / 6 mm all round. Using a water-soluble marker, mark the precise edge of the pattern over the pieces of cut organza. With the kimono *right side out*, pin and tack / baste each piece of organza in the correct position.

Below left. *Detail from the larger front motif. The lines of machine stitching which enclose the butterflies under the organza overlay show up clearly.*

Below right. *Enlarge the 3 pieces of the overlay pattern 400%. Use the enlarged pattern pieces to cut the organza and the Stitch 'n' Tear shapes.*

7. Using a straight machine stitch and Madeira Rayon 2001 thread, machine each piece of organza in place, following the marked line. Still using a straight machine stitch with Madeira Rayon 2004 thread, carefully stitch around the contours of each butterfly (see photographic detail below). The silk butterflies are now caught between the kimono fabric and the organza and will not fray. The ends of the threads should be tied off and neatly sewn by hand into the back of the work.

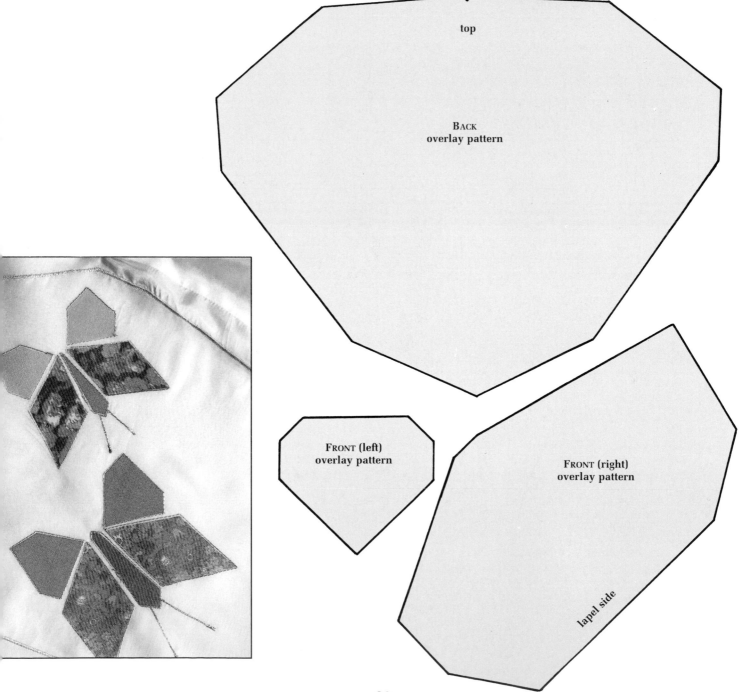

top

BACK
overlay pattern

FRONT (left)
overlay pattern

FRONT (right)
overlay pattern

lapel side

8. The butterflies' antennae are worked in free-machine embroidery (see page 110, paragraph 6), also in Madeira Rayon 2004, using a small embroidery hoop to keep each section taut as it is worked on. If you wish, you can mark the antennae on the fabric with the marker pen first.

9. Very carefully, trim the raw edge of the silk organza, close to the line of stitching. With a medium-width satin stitch and using Madeira Rayon 2001, stitch over the original line of straight stitching which attached the organza overlay to the kimono, enclosing it as well as the raw edge of the organza. Again, carefully tie off and sew in the ends of the machine threads.

10. The tear-off backing material has now fulfilled its function, which was to hold the layers flat and give them body while the machine-stitching and embroidery was carried out. Tear it off carefully, using tweezers if necessary, to take out the fragments trapped in the stitching. Press.

The butterfly decoration can also be used on a pyjama jacket or indeed on a shirt. The shape and size of the organza overlays can easily be changed or reduced.

The appliqued overlay at the back of the kimono. The layer of organza mutes the colours of the butterflies and creates a delicate moire effect over the applique.

COURT JESTER'S BAG

Jill Essery

Opposite page. *The finished bag is 9½ in /
25 cm high. A partially completed
diamond is reproduced in front of it.*

Diagram 1., below. *The base of the bag
is hexagonal. The diamonds are folded
over along the dotted line to form the
base of the bag. The letters indicate the
colour sequence.*

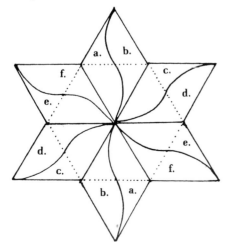

This little bag uses a form of Japanese folded patchwork. Each shape consists of a circle made of 2 differently coloured halves, pieced together. The circle is then folded into a diamond and when the diamonds are joined to each other with an insertion stitch, the folded edges form long serpentine curves at the sides of the bag. Each diamond encloses its own piece of wadding / batting and the decorative running stitch which holds the diamond together is a form of self-quilting. As each shape is folded in on itself, the back of the patch is as neat as the front and does not require lining. By a careful choice of colours and tones, the serpentine curve within each diamond is followed through the adjoining ones, so that there is a counterpoint of diamond and sinuous vertical patterns.

1. Enlarge the 3 templates on page 67, as instructed. Make cardboard masters. Use **template 3.** to cut 6 diamond-shaped pieces of wadding / batting. Use **template 1.** to cut 2 half circles of each of your 6 fabrics. Arrange 6 of the half circles in pairs of sympathetic colours. Repeat the same colour combinations for the remaining 6 half circles. Assign a reference letter to each colour within the pairs. (The 1st pair, which might be yellow and orange, should be A and B, and so on.) This will help you to maintain the correct colour sequence later on. Machine-stitch the centre of each circle. Press. These 6 circles will form the initial 6 diamonds, which are the base of the bag. The sketches on page 67 show how to proceed from circles to finished diamonds (**template 2.** is the ironing template). NOTE: the base of the bag requires additional firmness, therefore you must cut 6 pelmet-weight Vilene shapes (use **template 3.**), splitting them in half, as marked, to help with the folding of the sides of the bag. These pieces should be inserted *under* the wadding / batting. Complete these 6 diamonds, as instructed. Use coton perlé in colours which tone with each piece to quilt the diamonds.

2. **Assembling the base of the bag.** Refer to **diagram 1.** opposite and position the diamonds following the colour sequence. Join, using an insertion stitch (see **diagram 4.** on page 16) and toning coton perlé.

3. **Diagram 2.** on page 66 shows the arrangement and colour sequence over the *entire* bag. You have already completed row 1 (the base of the bag). Now prepare 6 diamonds, identical in colour to the ones you made for the base. They

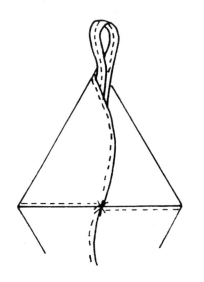

Diagram 2. *The positioning of the diamonds over the entire bag and the colour sequence, identified by letters. The bottom row is already complete and forms the base of the bag.*

This sketch shows how the loop has been inserted into the top of one of the diamonds in the 3rd row (the top of the bag). It explains why the quilting of these diamonds had to be left incomplete (paragraph 3.)

Opposite a. *Preparing a tassel, using thin rouleau. In **b.** a short length of bias strip is wrapped around the top of the tassel to simulate a knot. A few stitches hold it in place.*

will form the top of the bag – row 3. NOTE: when quilting these diamonds, do not complete the stitching at the uppermost points. Leave about 1 in / 2.5 cm open, with the thread hanging loose, to be completed *after* you insert the turquoise loops. Row 2. also consists of 6 diamonds, but the colours have been rearranged. Use the letters to guide you. Join up rows 2. and 3. with the insertion stitch as before. Refer to the diagram of the base of bag and fold the diamonds along the dotted line. Attach the lower edge of row 2. to the base of the bag, still using the insertion stitch. Work the insertion stitch along the open side to close up the bag.

4. Out of the contrasting fabric (I used turquoise), cut 6 bias strips 1⅛ x 4 in / 2.8 x 10 cm. Press in half lengthwise, and turn the edges in to the centre fold to form a folded bias binding. Use contrasting coton perlé to work a small running stitch down the centre of each strip. Fold each in half to make a loop and insert into the top of each diamond. Make sure all the loops are the same length. Sew firmly into place, using ordinary sewing thread. Complete the quilting stitch to the top of the diamonds (see sketch opposite).

5. **The cord handles**. Out of the largest piece of remaining silk, cut 2 bias strips each 1½ x 33 in / 3.8 x 84 cm, joining if necessary. Make 2 lengths of rouleau, using No. 2 piping cord (refer to instructions of page 123).

6. **The tassels**. These are made of thinner rouleau. The bias strips are 1⅛ in /2.8 cm wide this time. Cut short bias strips in as many colours as possible, joining them to make a total length of 14 in / 36 cm for each tassel. Make up the rouleau as before, but using No. 0 piping cord. Coil the length of rouleau to form 4 loops and catch them at the top with a few stitches. Attach to the end of the cord handle. Wrap a short length of bias strip to hide the raw edges and form the head of the tassel. Slip-stitch to hold (see sketch at the bottom of the page). Make 3 more tassels. Thread the handles through the loops in opposite directions.

7. **Holding rings**. Out of the contrasting silk, cut 2 3 in / 7.5 cm lengths of bias strip and prepare as in paragraph 4. Wrap around the paired ends of the cord handles, just above the tassels. They should be loose enough to slide up and down the handles, but tight enough to prevent the tassels from coming through. Close the ends neatly with a few stitches.

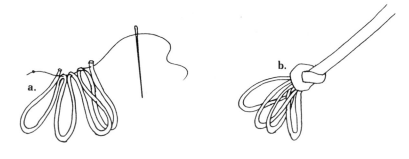

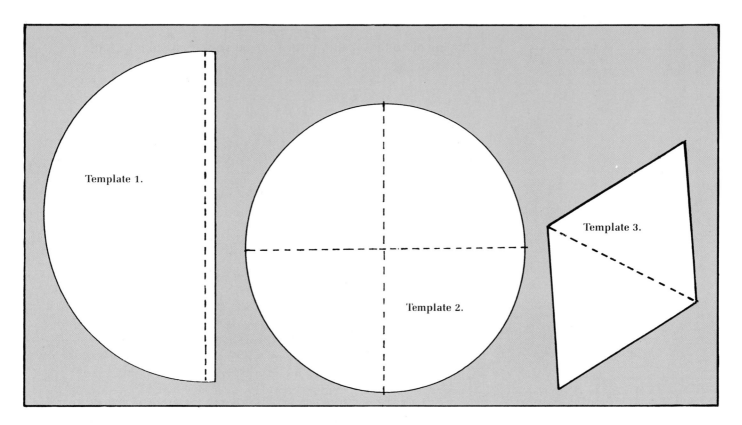

Template 1. *Use to cut 2 half circles of each of your 6 fabrics. Join along dotted line. Run a line of gathers close to the edge of the circle (see step **1.** on page 118).*

Template 2. *Mark the dotted lines on this ironing template. When inserting it inside the slightly gathered up circle, ensure that the vertical on the template aligns with the seam joining the 2 half circles. Tighten the gathering thread and press the edge. Remove the template.*

Template 3. *Use to cut 24 diamond-shaped pieces of wadding / batting. Cut along the dotted line to obtain 12 pelmet-weight Vilene triangles to reinforce the base of the bag. To form the folded diamonds follow the sketches **a.** to **c.** on the right.*

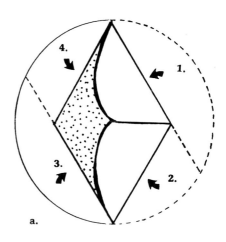

Turning circles into diamonds. Place **template 3.** over the wrong side of the circle, aligning the vertical with the seam joining the half circles. Fold the cloth over the template (shaded area in sketch **a.**), in the order marked. Press. Remove template. Insert wadding / batting triangle. Work a running stitch, using coton perlé (see sketch **b.** which shows the front of the diamond). The stitch not only holds the diamond together but quilts it at the same time. Sketch **c.** shows the back of the diamond. A partly quilted example was photographed next to the finished bag on page 65.

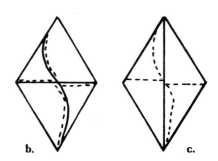

TUDOR-STYLE BODICE

Gilly Wraight

This unusual top can be worn by itself or over a long-sleeved shirt. The technique used is crazy patchwork, partly made on the machine as explained on page 113 and partly hand-finished. This means that some of the edges of the patches have been folded over and held in position over the neighbouring piece with a hand-made running stitch or a herringbone stitch. This form of crazy patchwork was very popular in the 19th century, but the edges of the fabric were left raw and the embroidery carried out over them. The material tended to fray, which does not happen when you fold the edge over, as I have done here. It also adds texture and interest to the work, yet it is quick and easy. The bodice is embellished with ruched silk rosettes, beads and shells. The back is made of plain toning material and the whole garment is cotton-lined.

The pattern fits a US size 8, UK 10, European 38.

1. Enlarge the back pattern on page 71 and make a paper master. Repeat for the front but make 2 sets – 1 will be used to cut the foundation fabric and the lining of the bodice, the other will be cut up along the lines of the numbered templates of the patchwork.

2. Cut 2 front pieces out of the foundation fabric, 2 of lining. Cut 1 back out of the plain toning fabric and 1 of lining.

3. Lay the 2nd paper front pattern down on the table, numbers and arrows uppermost. Lay a piece of tracing paper over it and trace off all the patchwork shapes. Cut up both sets of templates. The tracing paper templates will be used in reverse so that the 2 halves of the front of the garment echo each other (refer to photographs). Transfer the numbers and the arrows to the back of the tracing paper templates.

4. Using the 2 sets of prepared templates, cut out the silk pieces, allowing for a ¼ in / 6 mm seam allowance all round. Lay out the cut pieces as you go along and plan the colour combination carefully. The fronts of the bodice mirror each other as far as patchwork *shapes* are concerned, but not necessarily in the colours. I arranged these randomly.

5. Fold under and tack / baste all the edges which are marked with curved arrows on the pattern. The others will be machine-stitched, following the instructions on page 113. Fix shape 1 on to the foundation fabric and continue up to piece no. 31.

SHOPPING LIST

40 in / 1 m white cotton lawn 36 in / 90 cm wide (foundation fabric)
4 pieces 10 in / 25 cm slub silk in different colours
scraps of silk in other weights and textures and in various colours
40 in / 1 m toning cotton fabric to line the bodice
23½ in / 60 cm plain cotton or silk fabric for the back of the bodice (to tone in with patchwork)
24 in / 60 cm narrow ribbon
beads and shells
embroidery silk threads – contrasting and toning colours
fabric bonding adhesive
toning machine-sewing thread
6 large hook and eye fastenings
tracing paper

Embroidery stitches used on the bodice.
a. *Single threaded running stitch*
b. *Double running stitch*
c. *Herringbone stitch*
d. *French knots*
e., f. *Backstitch wheel or spider*
Also see the stitch diagrams on page 22.

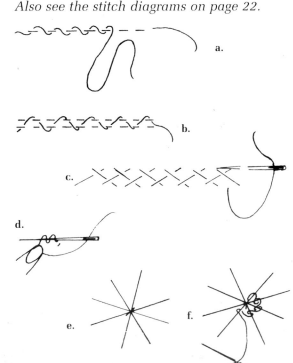

6　Use the adhesive (sparingly) to hold pieces 32, 33 and 34 into place over the foundation fabric. Machine the pieces with a zigzag machine stitch and couch the narrow ribbon by hand over the line of stitching. Work a herringbone stitch or a running stitch over the tacked / basted seams, using a variety of colours and thicknesses of embroidery threads. Remove tacking / basting stitches. Press.

7. Work the darts into the fronts of the bodice. Attach the beads and the shells firmly, using strong silk thread.

8. Work the darts into the back of the garment and into the lining, front and back.

9. **Assembling the bodice.** Pin or tack / baste the finished fronts of the bodice to the back. Machine-stitch. Trim and press seams. Join the fronts and the back of the lining in the same way. Try on the garment to ensure that it fits and alter darts slightly (in the lining too) if necessary. Place the lining, right side down, on the right side of the bodice. Tack / baste and machine-stitch the front, neck and lower edge seams. Turn the garment right side out through one of the unstitched armholes. Press.

10. Trim seam allowance and make notches around the curve of the armholes. Turn the fabric inward and work 2 rows of machine top-stitching around the armholes. Fix the hooks and eyes firmly into place, in such a way that the 2 halves of the front of the body meet flush. The large hooks can be stitched on the top of the right-hand side of the front of the garment, as they will be hidden by the silk rosettes.

11. **Ruched rosettes.** Enlarge the rosette template on page 71. From the remaining silk fabrics, cut 14 or more circles and prepare as shown below. I have used 6 at the centre front of the bodice, 5 to outline the front of each armhole, there is 1 at the centre of the neck at the back and 3 more have been distributed randomly on the front of the garment, near the darts. The size of the rosettes varies, depending on how tightly you pull the gathering thread. Attach them with a few invisible stitches around the circumference, then scrunch up the centre, fixing the fabric with a few more stitches.

Previous page. *The finished bodice. The shimmering silks give great richness to its autumnal colours.*

Above. *A detail from the front of the bodice, showing the ruched rosettes.*

Left. *Making a rosette. Enlarge the template on page 71, opposite. Make a master. Mark and make a hole at each dot to enable you to mark the pattern on to the cut circles of silk, using a quilting pencil. Turn over the raw edge of the circle down to the outside dots. Run a gathering thread along the drawn pattern as shown in the example on the left. Draw the thread and secure it. Slip-stitch the ruched circle to the garment.*

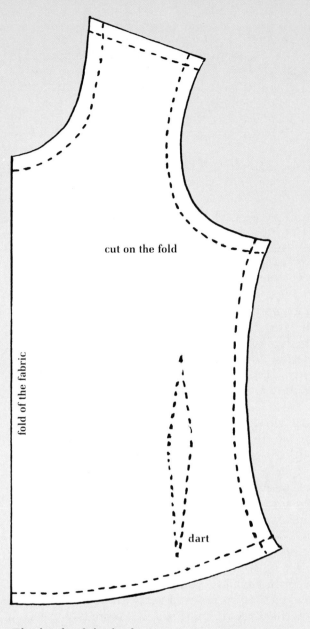

cut on the fold

fold of the fabric

dart

The back of the bodice

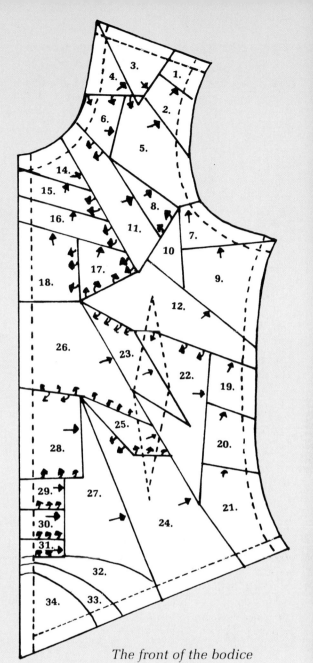

1.
2.
3.
4.
5.
6.
7.
8.
9.
10.
11.
12.
14.
15.
16.
17.
18.
19.
20.
21.
22.
23.
24.
25.
26.
27.
28.
29.
30.
31.
32.
33.
34.

The front of the bodice

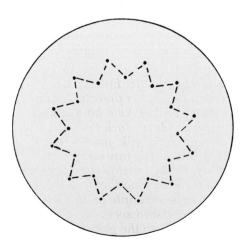

Above. Enlarge the pattern for the bodice 400%. The dotted lines are the sewing lines. Note the darts at the back and the front of the garment. These may need to be adjusted to fit you. Make individual templates of the patches, as described in paragraphs 3. to 5. on page 68, not forgetting to add a 1/4 in / 6 mm seam allowance around each patch.

Left. Enlarge the template for the ruched rosettes 200%. Use as explained at the bottom of page 70.

ENGLISH PATCHWORK SILK PURSE

Christine Donaldson

This attractive evening bag is made of shot silk dupion and worked in English patchwork. A shot fabric is one in which the warp threads are of one colour and the weft of another. This causes the cloth to change colour, depending on the position of the fabric and the way in which the light falls on it. By changing the direction of the grain of the fabric, interesting effects can be created, as this piece shows. The bag has been embellished with tiny beads and tassels. Worked in matching fabrics, it would be the perfect accompaniment to a bridesmaid's outfit, or indeed to the wedding dress itself.

Basic instructions for English patchwork appear on page 114.

1. Using the inner portion of the template shown on page 74, make an accurate cardboard master and use it to trace and cut out 192 paper triangles.

2. Using the outer dimensions of the template, make an accurate cardboard master. Use it to mark and cut out 96 triangles with the grain running *vertically* and 96 *horizontally*. Dupion silk frays easily, so handle the pieces as little and as gently as possible.

3. Pin and tack / baste the fabric pieces to the paper templates and arrange the patches by alternating the direction of the grain carefully, as shown in the sketch on page 74. Work in a good light and check that the grain runs in the desired direction all the time, or your final piece of work will be ruined. It is helpful to pin the patches to a cork board or a piece of polystyrene before you start sewing.

4. Make up the 2 panels of patchwork (the front and back of the bag). Press the completed patchwork on the wrong side and then, placing the two halves right sides together, oversew them together and up to the crosses shown on the diagram, leaving the top of the bag open.

5. Enlarge the pattern on page 74 and use it to cut 2 pieces of the contrasting silk to form the lining. Stitch together between the dots. Trim the corners and the seams to ¼ in / 6 mm, sloping it out to the full ⅝ in / 15 mm seam allowance at the dots shown at the sides of the pattern.

6. Slip the lining inside the patchwork purse, wrong sides facing and matching up the side seams. Turn the top raw

Opposite page. The finished purse measures approximately 11 x 8½ in / 28 x 22.5 cm

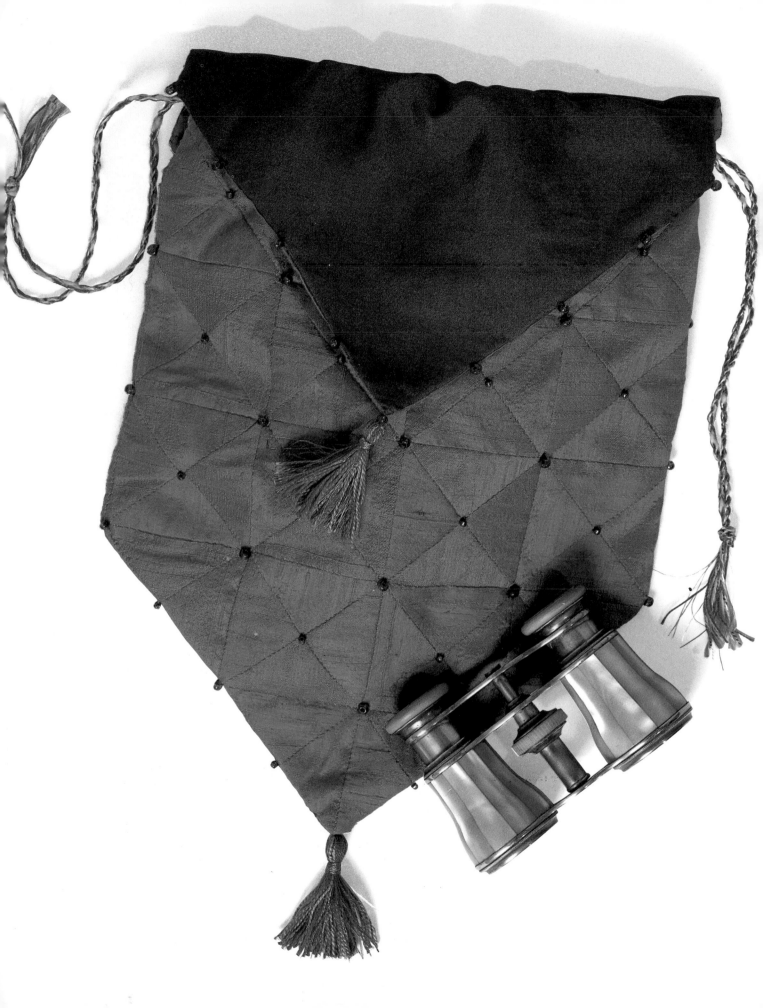

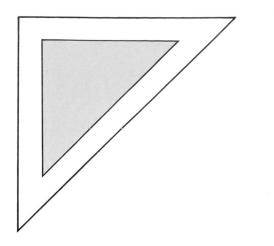

This template is reproduced life size.

Below left. *The arrows in this sketch show the grain direction of the shot silk. The dotted lines represent the stitching lines, ⅜ in / 10 mm apart, which form the channel for the drawstrings.*

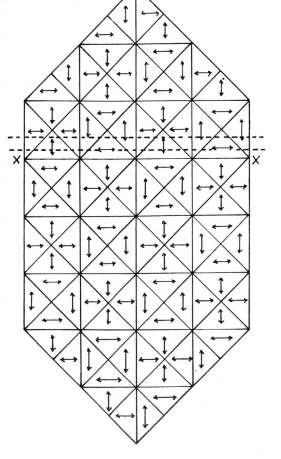

Join the 2 lower sections of
the bag, starting at the crosses

edges of the lining in by ⅝ in / 15 mm (the same width as the seam allowance), pin and tack / baste to meet the edge of the patchwork. Stitch the edges of the lining and the patchwork together with tiny slip stitches. Leave an opening of 1 in / 25 mm on either side of the bag, above the side seams. Place the bag on the table, ensuring that the patchwork and the lining lie flat. Pin and tack / baste 2 lines of stitching as indicated on the diagram shown on the left, below. Machine-stitch along these or do it by hand, using a back stitch. This forms the channel for the drawstring. Close up any small gaps below and above the channel opening, using tiny, invisible slip stitches. Remove tacking / basting.

7. Sew beads around the top edge of the bag and at the intersections of the diamonds formed by the patchwork, alternating the size of the beads (see the photograph of the purse on page 73). Attach the tassels to the ends of the flaps and the bottom of the bag.

8. Cut 2 lengths of cord 30 in / 76 cm long. Using a safety-pin, thread 1 through the channel running at the front of the bag. Repeat for the back. Tie the ends of the cord on either side, trim and 'fluff' out to make tassels.

lining
cut 2

straight grain of the fabric

Right. *Enlarge this pattern 400% and use it to cut the lining. The pattern includes a ⅝ in / 15 mm seam allowance.*

APPLIQUED 'KAMA' QUILT

Gisela Thwaites

I gave the name of the Hindu God of Love to this quilt, inspired by a motif found on the cenotaph under the central cupola of the Taj Mahal, which was built by Emperor Shah Jahan as a symbol of his undying love for his wife, Mumtaz. The shimmering white marble is inlaid with a variety of semi-precious stones: carnelian, jade, onyx, turquoise. I chose the fabrics very carefully to match the subtle shades of the original. The entire piece was worked in hand applique and hand-quilted.

1. Enlarge the drawing on page 78. It will later be used to produce templates, see 2. below, but first copy it on to tracing paper twice right way up and twice in reverse to obtain the entire circular pattern. Go over the whole pattern with a black marker to get a really clear outline. Tape it to a flat surface. Fold the piece of background material in half, press and fold again to find the true centre. Press. Tape the background fabric over the drawing, right side up. With a sharp hard pencil transfer the whole of the design lightly over the material. (I mark just *inside* the lines to make sure nothing shows when the applique is in place.)

2. Using the enlarged drawing mentioned above, cut card templates of the various flowers (individual petals), leaves, 'sunray' shapes and of the bosses – the small circular shapes immediately inside the 'sunray' pattern. Use the photographs of the quilt and of the central motif on page 77 to guide you in the choice of colours. The narrow curving brown lines are produced with bias strips. Do not make templates of these, the process involved is described in 7. overleaf.

3. Silk frays easily, so cut up the individual motifs as you need them and applique as you go. I have used the freezer paper method in which you use the prepared templates to trace the shapes on to the *shiny* side of the freezer paper with the *right* side of the pattern facing you. Cut out these shapes along the drawn line. Place the cut-out

The finished quilt measures 48 in / 122 cm square.

75

freezer-paper shapes on the *wrong side* of the fabric, and with the dull side of the paper facing up. Press (do not use a steam iron). Cut out the shapes, allowing ¼ in / 6 mm for turnovers. Tack / baste this seam allowance over the edge of the freezer paper.

4. Start with the large marguerite at the very centre of the quilt. Prepare the individual petals, flower centre etc, as explained above. Place one dark petal over the pale one. The dark petal should *just* overlap the edge of the light petal. Join with small slip stitches. Make the stitches fairly tight, without distorting the shape of the petals. When the 16 outer petals are assembled, repeat the process for the 8 small turquoise-coloured shapes. Slip-stitch the centre. Place this central rosette over the centre of the prepared outer petals. Slip-stitch into position. Using the same method, work the leaves and the lily-shaped flowers, which radiate from the central marguerite. Slip-stitch these motifs on to the marked background fabric. Remove the tacking / basting, then the freezer paper by making little slits at the back of the applique. Lift the paper out with a pin. The stems are worked in chain stitch, using the pale green coton à broder.

5. Out of the metallic printed fabric, cut 100 'sunray' shapes and prepare them, as described above. Applique them on to the background fabric, with small slip stitches.

6. The freezer-paper method is not used for the bosses. Instead, place the prepared card template (make a few duplicates) over the *wrong* side of the coloured silk. Trace around the template with a quilting pencil. Cut out the circular shapes, allowing ¼ in / 6 mm for turnovers. You'll want 17 of each of the 4 darker shades of silks. Run a line of gathers between the drawn outline and the edge of the fabric. Place templates inside and tighten the gathering thread. Prepare a number of these bosses and press (do not use a steam iron). You can then pull out the templates and the bosses will keep their shape. Applique them on to the background fabric, as before.

7. **Using bias strips to produce narrow curvilinear shapes**. Out of the remaining carnelian-coloured silk, cut 6½ yd / 6 m of bias strips. This is done by folding the cloth diagonally against the selvage. Press the fold. Use a ruler to draw lines, parallel to the fold and 1¼ in / 30 mm apart. Cut and steam-iron in half, wrong sides together. Lay the raw edge of the strip over the line you wish to cover, ease round the curve so that it lies smoothly. Pin into position. Machine-stitch ⅛ in / 3 mm away from the raw edge. When you reach a flower motif, which will be appliqued later, cut the strip, allowing ⅝ in / 15 mm to be tucked under the motif. Fold the strip over to cover the line of stitching. The finished width should be ½ in / 13 mm. Pin so that the strip lies smoothly and slip-stitch along the edge.

8. Prepare and applique all the remaining flowers etc, tucking the ends of the network of bias strips neatly under the

Opposite page. The front and the back of the central marguerite. The freezer paper templates show clearly at the back of the piece. The motif is now ready to be appliqued at the centre of the quilt. When this is done, the paper shapes must be removed as explained in paragraph 4.

Above. A detail of the centre of the quilt showing the lily motifs, the curvilinear shapes simulating the stems of the flowers, the sunrays and the bosses contained within 2 curving brown lines, made of bias strips (see end of paragraph 2.). Note how the straight and curving quilting lines outline the motifs or fill the spaces between them.

Below. Enlarge this drawing 400%. It shows a quarter section of the large roundel in the middle of the quilt and the marguerite which forms the very centre of the design.

motifs. Out of the remaining gold metallic printed fabric, cut 4½ yd / 4 m of 1 in / 26 mm wide bias strips. Repeat the process described in 8. above, and apply to the double circle, immediately inside the 'sunray' pattern. The finished width of this bias strip will be ¼ in / 6 mm. Embroider the narrow stems in chain stitch as before. As you can see from the picture, I outlined and highlighted most of the flowers and leaves in stem stitch, worked in gold thread, and attached small beads to some of the flowers. This is optional.

9. Using a ruler and a sharp hard pencil, draw a line 7 in / 18 cm away from the outer edge of the quilt. Do this along all 4 sides. Out of the remaining amber-coloured silk, cut strips along the grain of the fabric, 152 x 2 in / 380 x 5 cm. Join to make a continuous strip. Fold in half and press. Machine-stitch ¼ in / 6 mm from the edge, making sure the thread does not pull. Use a safety-pin to turn the strip inside out. Press flat. Applique over the drawn line with the width of the strip directed towards the centre of the quilt. Lay the ends of the strips over each other. Trim the raw edge of the underlying strip just inside the drawn line. Fold the raw edge of the upper strip over it, tuck the end neatly under and finish off with tiny slip stitches.

10. Lay the backing material face down on the floor. Place the wadding / batting over it and cover with the top of the quilt. Tack / baste the 3 layers together, as explained on page 121. Start quilting. I used outline quilting round the centre motif, up to the first 'circle'. This lifts the flowers slightly, making them stand out from the background. For the rest, I worked straight and curved lines ½ in / 13 mm apart (reduced to ¼ in / 6 mm towards the outer section of the quilt – refer to the photographs on page 77). I also worked 6 lines of quilting, ¼ in / 6 mm apart, outside the amber strip described in 9. above. Square off all 3 layers to the same size. Fold the edge of the top of the quilt (together with the wadding / batting) about 1 in / 25 mm. Do the same for the backing and attach the front to the back with small stitches.

BEADED & QUILTED PANEL 'PERSPECTIVE DREAMS'

Gilly Wraight

The silk used for this small panel was dyed in delicate hues of old pink and blue. It matches the bed cover shown on page 105. I based the motif on the grid devised by painters in the late medieval period, which enabled them to give their pictures a new feeling of realism by the introduction of perspective. In my piece, the 'dreams' are depicted with soft Suffolk puffs and tiny beads.

SHOPPING LIST

1 yd / 90 cm white habutai silk,
    45 in / 112 cm wide
½ yd / 45 cm lightweight (natural fibre)
    wadding / batting
machine-sewing thread in white,
    pale blue and 3 shades of pink
small beads
2 small curtain rings
2 pots of silk dye in pink and blue
    (no steam-fixing)
1 sponge brush
4 small dishes for the dye and water
quilting pencil

1. Enlarge the diagram on page 80, as instructed. This will become the pattern. Use it to cut 3 oblongs of fabric, adding 8 in / 20 cm all round. Cut 1 further piece, half the size of the other 3. Out of the wadding / batting, cut 3 oblongs 16½ x 11¾ in / 42 x 30 cm.

2. Take 1 of the large oblongs of silk. Using white thread, machine-stitch vertical lines freely, approximately ¾ in / 20 mm apart. Practise this first on an offcut of silk to find the right tension on the machine. Allow the fabric to glide freely through your hands, pulled only by the feed dogs of the machine. Stitch each line from the top and, before beginning the next line, run the row of stitches between finger and thumb to even out any puckers.

3. **Dyeing the silk**. Pour a small amount of blue dye in one of the dishes and dilute with a little water. Repeat for the pink dye. The 3rd dish is for mixing the colours. Have clean water ready, too. Pin the 4 silk pieces on to large sheets of clean paper which will absorb the excess dye. Stick the paper / silk pieces on to a flat surface with masking tape. Mark on the paper where the top of each piece will be. Using the sponge brush, dampen the silk sparingly with clean water. Experiment with the dyes on a spare piece of silk until you are satisfied with the shades of blue and pink. The sponge brush can be rinsed off quickly between colour applications and dried with kitchen paper.

4. The oblong with machine-stitchery will form the front of the panel, the 2nd large piece will form the back, so these should be dyed similarly and kept very light in colour. The 3rd larger piece is for making the Suffolk puffs – dye it darker than the previous 2. The remaining piece is for the triangular applique panel. Dye it darkest of all (see photograph for guidance). Write on the paper backing what each silk piece will be. Allow fabric to dry. Fix the dye, according to the manufacturer's instructions.

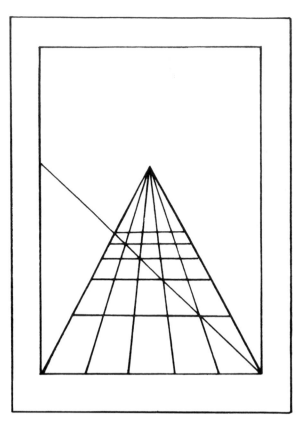

Above. Enlarge this pattern 400%.

Below. Making Suffolk puffs.

5. Transfer the pattern on to tracing paper. Tack / baste this tracing on to the smaller piece of dyed silk. Using blue thread, machine-stitch *through the paper* and along the vertical lines and the outline of the pyramid. When the stitching is complete, tear the paper from the top along a ruler's edge to avoid pulling out the machine-stitches. Refer to the master plan and, using the quilting pencil, trace the 5 horizontal lines on to the pyramid. Machine-stitch these lines in turn, using blue thread.

6. Take the front of the hanging (see 2. above) and position the pyramid over it. The front piece is much larger than the finished wallhanging. This is to allow you to choose the area where the dye is most successful. Check with the pattern that you are positioning the pyramid properly in relation to the rest of the piece. Tack / baste. Make another tracing of the pattern, but cut away the border, keeping only the central panel. Pin this over the front of the hanging and tack / baste it over one of the pieces of wadding / batting. Run several rows of machine-stitching along the edges of the inner panel, using blue thread. Cut away the excess wadding / batting beyond this line. Remove the paper.

7. Position the original pattern over the front of the hanging. Match the corners of the inner panel and pin through the paper. Match the outer corners of the hanging and mark with pins. Take the 2 remaining pieces of batting / wadding and attach them to each other with a few stitches. Tack / baste them to the back of the panel.

8. **The Suffolk puffs**. Out of the 3rd large piece of dyed silk, cut 2 circles 4 in / 10 cm in diameter, 2 3½ in / 9 cm, 5 3 in / 7.5 cm, 3 2¼ in / 6 cm, 12 2 in / 5 cm and 8 1¾ in / 4.5 cm. Turn ¼ in / 6 mm and run a gathering thread around the puff by hand. Pull the thread tight and secure it to form a little purse – flattened and with the gathered side uppermost. It will form 1 puff (see partly worked examples opposite). Plan how you are going to distribute the puffs over the design and, where they touch each other, attach them first, then applique them over the hanging. This requires only a few tiny stitches. Lastly attach the beads.

9 **Assembling the wallhanging.** Put the piece, face down, on the table. Trim off the excess fabric ⅝ in / 15 mm away from the edge of the wadding / batting layer. Turn the piece over so that it faces up and place the remaining dyed oblong of silk – the backing of the hanging – over it. Trim off excess cloth. Machine-stitch just outside the edge of the wadding / batting, leaving one short side open to turn the piece right side out. Slip-stitch this gap shut. Attach 2 small curtain rings just below the top corners of the wallhanging so that they do not show when the piece is on the wall. The panel is now complete.

Opposite page. *The finished panel measures 16¼ x 12 in / 42 x 30 cm.*

STENCILLED & APPLIQUED FLOOR CUSHION

Christine Donaldson

SHOPPING LIST

1½ yd / 140 cm dark blue cotton sateen
(furnishing quality) 47 in / 120 cm
wide
12 in / 30 cm red furnishing damask
4 pieces of gold brocade fabric each
3 in / 76 mm square
9 in / 23 cm each of blue, green, yellow
(gold) furnishing brocades or
damasks 47 in / 120 cm wide
1¼ yd / 114 cm of ½ in / 13 mm wide
gold braid
3 yd / 2.75 m of ¼ in / 6 mm diameter
gold cord
1 x 2 oz / 50 g ball of double-knit
cotton – yellow / gold
metallic gold embroidery thread
3 large buttons
scraps of brightly coloured silks for the
applique picture
paper-backed fusible web
toning sewing threads
1 x 26 in / 66 cm square cushion pad
cotton knitting yarn and metallic
thread

For the stencilling:
oiled manilla paper or acetate 3 in /
76 mm square
permanent fabric paint – gold
small piece of sponge or stencil brush

Opposite page. *The finished cushion measures 26 in / 66 cm square.* **Below.** *The stencil is reproduced life size. Cut out the shaded part.*

This truly regal cushion was inspired by the lavishness of medieval manuscripts. The blue background is stencilled with a gold flower motif and the American patchwork borders are made up of richly brocaded fabrics. Suppliers of ecclesiastical fabrics and trimmings are an excellent source of these materials.

The patchwork seam allowance is ¼ in / 6 mm, but it is ⅝ in / 15 mm on the outer edges of the border to allow for the making up of the cushion.

1. Transfer the stencilling pattern below to the oiled manilla paper or acetate and cut it out with a sharp craft knife.

2. Cut a piece of blue cotton sateen 10½ in / 27 cm square. This includes a ¼ in / 6 mm seam allowance all around. Avoiding stencilling within the seam allowance, decorate the panel with the flower motif. You will achieve a more pleasing result if you turn the stencil a little each time you place it on the fabric. You can mark the position of the stencil on the fabric beforehand, but with a little initial practice on a scrap of fabric, it is easy to do it freehand.

3. Cut 4 pieces of the blue cotton sateen 5 x 27½ in / 127 x 700 mm. Decorate these with the flower stencil, again avoiding stencilling within the seam allowance.

4. Allow the stencilling to dry and fix the colour according to the manufacturer's instructions.

5. Make templates for the applique picture, using the shapes on page 85. Make up out of brightly coloured silk scraps following the instructions for machine applique on page 120. Embroider ladybird's spots and butterfly's markings by hand or, as in the photograph, in free machine embroidery (see page 110, paragraph 6).

6. Cut 4 pieces of red damask 3 in / 76 mm x 10½ in / 27 cm. Pin and machine-stitch 2 of these, right sides together, on opposite sides of the central panel. Press the seams outwards from the centre. The usual practice in American patchwork is to press the seams away from the centre or towards the darker fabric to prevent the seam allowance showing through. As this cushion is made from thick, opaque furnishing fabrics you can press the seams in the direction in which they lie flattest.

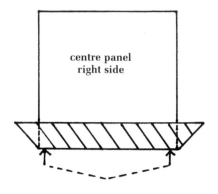

Diagram 1. Begin and end seam ¼ in / 6 mm from the edges of the panel.

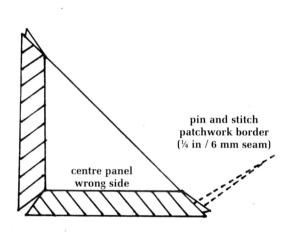

Diagram 2.

Opposite page. Enlarge the sketch shown bottom left 400%. The different sections of the applique are numbered. The corresponding individual templates are shown life size. The broken lines indicate where one shape fits under another.

7. Cut 4 squares of gold brocade fabric 3 in / 76 mm square. Pin and stitch them at each end of the 2 remaining red fabric strips. Press seams to one side. Pin and machine-stitch these strips to the remaining 2 sides of the central panel, matching seams and pressing to one side.

8. Make a card template, using the diamond shape on page 85. Cut 8 diamonds each out of the green, blue, red and yellow brocades. Make up 4 strips of patchwork, each consisting of 8 diamonds, starting with a green one (refer to the photograph of the cushion). Press all the seams in the same direction.

9. Lay the central panel of the cushion on a flat surface, right side up. Place a strip of patchwork (right sides facing) along the lower edge of the panel, matching edges and with the left-hand edge of the green diamond matching that of the panel. Pin and machine-stitch together, beginning and ending seam ¼ in / 6 mm from the edges of the panel. (See **diagram 1.** on the left.) Repeat along the other 3 sides of the panel.

10. **To form mitred corners**. Fold the central panel diagonally with right sides together and work a line of stitching across the patchwork border, following the line of the fold. Trim the excess patchwork from the seam allowance. Repeat for each corner. Press flat.

11. Repeat the process from stage 9, this time using the stencilled strips of blue cotton sateen. Cut one end of each strip at an angle of 45° and join to the main panel as before, angling the second end once in position. Stitch and press seams open. Stitch the ½ in / 13 mm gold braid around the inside of the appliqued central panel.

12. Cut a piece of blue cotton sateen the same width as the completed cushion top and 10 in / 254 mm longer. Fold this in half with the shorter sides together and cut along the fold. Stitch a ½ in / 13 mm hem along 1 long side of each piece. Lay the two pieces of fabric over the cushion front, right sides together, overlapping them in the centre. Pin and stitch the back to the front, using a ⅝ in / 15 mm seam. Trim the corners and turn right side out. Make 3 buttonholes on the outer half of the cushion back. Sew buttons.

13. Sew gold cord around the outer edge of the cushion, making a small gap in the centre of the seam on the lower edge of the cushion in which to tuck and fasten the ends of the cord.

14. Make 4 tassels, using cotton knitting yarn and metallic embroidery thread and winding the yarns around a piece of stiff card 4 in / 10 cm wide (see instructions on page 124). Attach firmly to the corners of the cushion. It is important for these tassels to be nice and fat. The cotton yarn, being matt, provides an interesting contrast with the richness of the cushion.

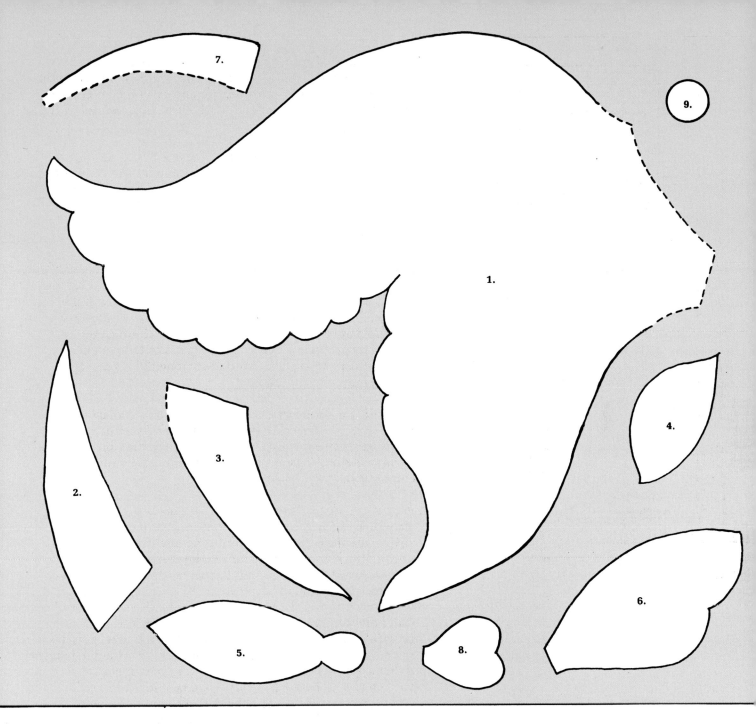

7.

9.

1.

4.

3.

2.

6.

5.

8.

Above. *Templates for the applique panel.*

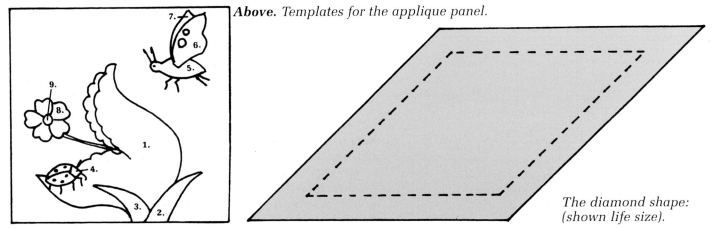

*The diamond shape:
(shown life size).*

BEADED EVENING BAG

Christine Donaldson

Cathedral window patchwork gives a nice textured surface to this bag, inspired by the sleeves of Elizabethan gowns. Large carnelian beads have been sewn at the intersections of the diamond shapes. What better use for that broken necklace which was never restrung?

SHOPPING LIST

1 yd / 90 cm silk dupion 44 in / 112 cm wide
9 in / 25 cm contrasting fabric (silk or other) for small squares, 36 in / 90 cm wide
12 in / 30 cm pelmet-weight interlining (Vilene)
8 in / 20 cm iron-on lightweight interlining (Vilene)
5 in / 13 cm lightweight zip fastener
39 large beads
1 Velcro tab
toning threads
button thread matching the beads

1. **The patchwork panel**. Make a cardboard template 6 in / 153 mm square. Cut 20 squares for the bag and 4 for the purse out of the main fabric (include a ¼ in / 6 mm seam allowance).

2. Using the template opposite, cut 31 centre squares for the bag and 4 for the purse out of the contrasting fabric.

3. Following the instructions for cathedral window patchwork on page 118, make up a panel 4 squares wide by 5 deep. The resulting piece of patchwork will form the front and back of the bag. Press.

4. Cut a piece of pelmet-weight interlining 10 x 18½ in / 25 x 47 cm. Attach the patchwork panel to the interlining by folding ¼ in / 6 mm of the edge of the patchwork over the edge of the interlining and holding it into place with small herringbone stitches. Start with one of the small dimensions of the patchwork, then work one of the long dimensions. Trim the width of the interlining if necessary and complete the second long side, leaving the fourth side open. Press. Using the button thread, attach 32 beads at the intersections of the patchwork pattern.

5. Fold the patchwork panel in half. The finished end will form the edge of the front flap of the bag. Make sure the patchwork lies smoothly over the interlining after folding. It should not pull. Tack/baste the open end of the patchwork onto the interlining. Cut a piece of your main fabric 10 x 5¾ in / 255 x 147 mm. Turn over ¼ in / 6 mm along one of the long dimensions. Pin over the line of tacking/basting at the bottom end of the bag and top-machine-stitch close to the edge of the folded fabric. Fold along this line of stitching and close the bag. The base of the front flap should lie flush with the bottom edge. Trim the open edge of the interlining so that the inside flap is 5½ in / 140 mm deep. Tack / baste the side edges of the fabric onto the interlining, but do not turn the edges over yet. With the bag folded, turn the fabric over the open front edge, tack / baste in position and top-machine-stitch close to the edge.

Use this template (shown life size) to cut the centre squares of the patchwork.

Opposite page. *The finished bag measures approximately 6 x 10 in / 15½ x 25½ cm and the purse 5 x 3 in / 13 x 7.5 cm.*

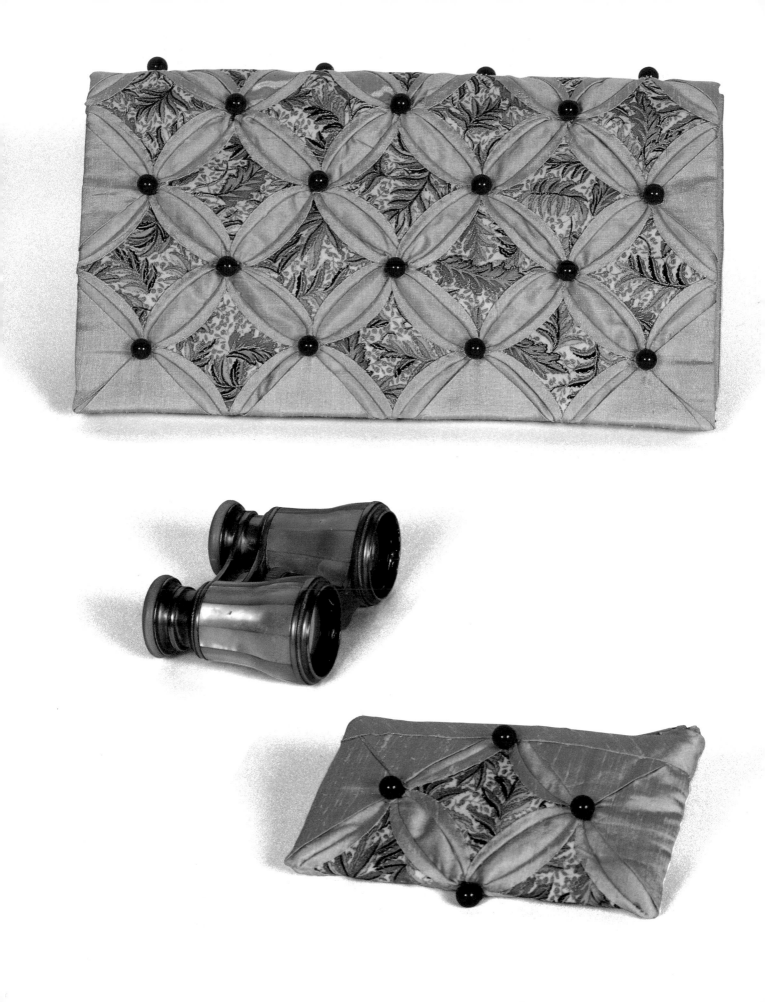

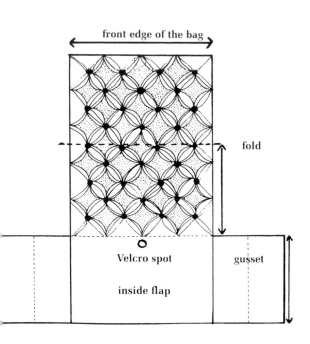

front edge of the bag

fold

Velcro spot gusset

inside flap

In this sketch showing the right side of the bag, the broken lines represent the folding lines. The remaining open long dimension of each gusset (marked by an arrow) must be slip-stitched to the inside of the back of the bag (marked by an arrow).

6. **Lining the bag**. Cut a piece out of the main fabric 10½ x 18 in / 27 x 46 cm. Turn over ¼ in / 6 mm along one short and one long side. Press. Slip-stitch to the inside front edge of the patchwork and along one side until you reach the inside flap of the bag, i.e. the end of the patchwork panel. Trim excess fabric if necessary and repeat on the other side.

7. **The gussets**. Cut 4 pieces of silk 6 x 4 in / 153 x 102 mm. Line 2 with iron-on interlining. Join 1 unlined with 1 lined piece, right sides together. Machine-stitch on 4 sides, ¼ in / 6 mm from the edge, leaving a small opening to turn over. Press. Slip-stitch opening. Top-machine-stitch close to the edge along 1 of the shorter sides. This will form the top of the gusset. Fold in half along the long side. Repeat for second gusset.

8. Lay one of the long sides of the prepared gusset over the right side of the inside flap of the bag. Machine-stitch ¼ in / 6 mm from the edge, flush with the interlining. Fold gusset into position. Press. Slip-stitch to hold fold so that the inner edge of the gusset is fixed to the lining and the interlining. Take care that the stitches do not come through the front of the flap. Repeat for second gusset. Holding the bag folded, pin the loose side of the gusset to the inside of the back of the bag. Slip-stitch into position. It is a little tricky as you come towards the bottom fold of the bag. Pull the inside base of the gusset and secure with a few stitches which can be hidden in the line of stitching at the base of the bag. Repeat for the other gusset. Press. Fix the furry part of the Velcro tab at the centre of the front flap of the bag, with tiny slip stitches, ¼ in / 6 mm from the edge. Fix the other half of the tab at the centre of the base of the inside flap, ⅜ in / 10 mm from the edge.

9. **The purse**. Assemble 4 cathedral window squares. Cut 2 strips out of the main fabric, each 1 x 5½ in / 25 x 140 mm. Fold patchwork piece over. Machine-stitch the 2 strips along the patchwork edges which will form the top of the purse, allowing for a ¼ in / 6 mm seam. Slip-stitch the sides of the purse. Cut a piece of the heavy interlining 5 x 5½ in / 127 x 140 mm. Fold in half along the shorter dimension and insert into the purse. Attach to the patchwork with a few invisible stitches at the base of the purse. Fix the 7 beads.

10. Turn over the edge of the fabric so that the strips are ½ in / 13 mm wide. Press. The interlining should be ¼ in / 6 mm shorter than the height of the purse, otherwise the zip will not open smoothly. Slip-stitch the edge of the strip to the zip.

11. **Lining the purse**. Cut a piece of fabric (whichever is the strongest) 5¾ x 6¼ in / 145 x 160 mm. Fold in half along the shorter dimension. Machine-stitch both sides, ¼ in / 6 mm from the edge. Insert into the purse. Trim excess fabric and slip-stitch to the inside of the zip, over the previous line of stitching. Push the base of the lining into the bottom corners of the purse. Fix it with a few slip stitches.

CRAZY PATCHWORK QUILT 'AN INDIAN AFFAIR'

Gisela Thwaites

The finished quilt measures 56 x 59 in / 1.42 x 1.50 m.

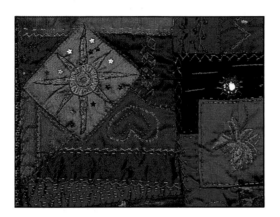

This quilt is made up of blocks of crazy patchwork. The elephants in the central panel are embroidered, but could also be appliqued. Two strips of 'secret garden' patchwork divide the rows of blocks. On page 92 you will find some of the motifs I embroidered on the various blocks. Enlarge them on the photocopier as instructed. The rest of the embroidery was done free-hand and the fabrics you use will suggest their own embellishments. See the paragraph headed **General principles** on page 20, and the instructions for attaching 'shishas' (Indian mirror pieces) on page 94. The beauty of crazy patchwork is that if you are not entirely happy with the juxtaposition of colours in one section, you can simply applique another patch over the offending area and cover the edges with herringbone or feather stitches. I use this method a lot. I also frequently overlap patches across 2 blocks. It breaks up the grid and creates interest.

1. At the top of page 92 you will find a cutting plan for the foundation material. Cut the blocks out of paper first and lay them over the fabric, according to the cutting plan. The sketch below identifies the individual blocks, and gives their *finished* measurements. The sizes which follow contain a seam allowance. Cut:
   10 blocks 12 in / 30 cm square (1.-5., 13.-17.)
   2 blocks 12 x 26 in / 30 x 66 cm (6., 12.)
   2 blocks 7½ x 26 in / 19 x 66 cm (7., 11.)
   1 block 16 x 26 in / 40 x 66 cm (9.)
   2 blocks 3½ x 26 in / 9 x 66 cm (8., 10.)

2. Refer to the instructions for crazy patchwork on page 113. I normally do all my patchwork by hand, but you may wish to do it on the machine. The working method is the same. Fill each block in turn and add whatever decoration or embroidery you deem necessary. I frequently add more after I have assembled the entire quilt. Beads, sequins and shishas can light up a dull area and simple embroidery can be picked out with beads, the printed pattern in the fabric outlined with gold thread, oddments of braid can be couched with coton à broder or narrow ribbon (see the picture of the small wall-hanging on page 45, for instance). You can also use gold fabric paint.

3. Embroider and decorate (or applique) the central 'elephant' panel. Tack / baste on to its piece of foundation material.

4. You have already cut 2 strips of foundation material for the strips on either side of the central panel. Cut 2 identical pieces out of the plain silk material. Tack / baste on top of the foundation fabric. Cover with embroidery, braid or flounced ribbon, or leave plain.

The sketch below shows the arrangement of the blocks within the quilt.

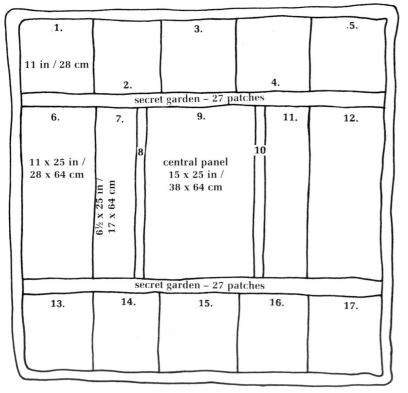

5. Referring to the sketch opposite, trim off each block to its finished size and, with right sides together, oversew block 1. to block 2., then block 2. to block 3. Continue until the first row is complete. Work the centre row in the same way and repeat for the bottom row. Cover the joins between the blocks with embroidery, couched ribbon etc.

6. Refer to instructions for 'secret garden' patchwork on page 120. Out of the gold metallic printed fabric, cut 54 squares, each measuring 5 in / 127 mm. Cut 54 2¼ in / 57 mm squares out of the contrasting fabric. Make up 2 strips of 27 squares, as per instructions, and insert between rows 1. and 2. and between rows 2. and 3. The top of the quilt is now complete but you can still add – or subtract – decoration. This is when my inexhaustible collection of bits comes into its own.

7. Lay the backing material face down on the floor. Place the batting / wadding over it and cover with the top of the quilt, right side up. Refer to quilting instructions on page 121. Tack / baste all 3 layers together. Quilt 'in the ditch' (preferably by hand), between the blocks. Square off the edges of the completed quilt.

8. **Binding and mitring the quilt**. Cut 9 strips, 6 x 36 in / 15 x 90 cm out of the plain or printed silk. Join them to make a continuous strip. Refer to instructions for binding and mitring a quilt on page 122.

The finished quilt in all its splendour. The elephants in the central panel were embroidered in chain stitch, using gold metallic thread. In India this type of embroidery is done with a tambour hook. I prefer doing it with a needle, in the European manner. The elephant motif could also be appliqued, with the main features picked out in embroidery.

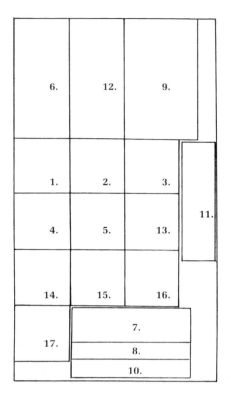

The cutting plan on the left shows how to position the various blocks on the calico foundation material. The elephant motifs above are shown 25% of their actual size; enlarge 400% to produce accurate templates. Enlarge the small motifs below 170% to get them to real size.

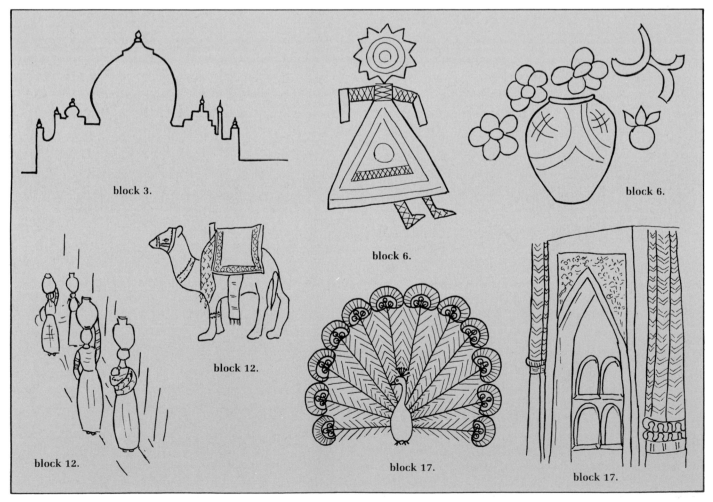

block 3.

block 6.

block 6.

block 12.

block 12.

block 17.

block 17.

CREAM SILK QUILT 'INDIAN REFLECTIONS'

Gisela Thwaites

This quilt was inspired by Indian miniatures with their glittering processions of elephants and white peacocks, and by the beautiful borders surrounding them. The top part of the quilt is appliqued with peacock motifs, quilted and embroidered. I used 'kantha' quilting, which comes from Bengal. The bottom section of the quilt, with the elephant border, was worked in the same way. The centre of the quilt is made of crazy patchwork, embellished with embroidery, beading and shisha work. I used a lot of loosely woven wild silk (mutka) which I embroidered with thick cotton thread or by pulled threadwork and beading. The top and bottom panels are outlined with narrow bands, embellished with shishas. The tassels are entirely made of tiny strips of silks, recycled from offcuts. It was wonderful to be able to use these marvellous fabrics, down to the smallest scraps.

The photographic detail below shows 1 of the appliqued peacocks, surrounded by 'kantha' quilting. A section of 1 of the shisha embroidery strips runs along the base of the picture.

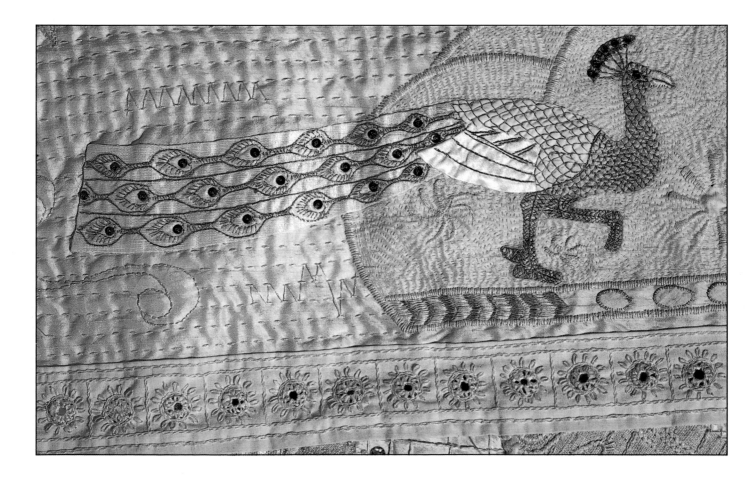

SHOPPING LIST

2½ yd / 2.30 m white calico, 45 in /
  115 cm wide for foundation material
  etc.
2 yd / 1.80 m white backing fabric,
  54 in / 140 cm wide
1 yd / 90 cm cream-coloured silk
  dupion, 45 in / 115 cm wide for
  appliqued panels
20 in / 50 cm each of white and grey
  silks, 36 in / 90 cm wide
1½ yd / 1.40 m cream-coloured habutai
  silk, 36 in / 90 cm wide for border
wide selection of white to cream to
  pale yellow silks in a variety of
  weights and textures, also heavy
  wild silk (mutka), fine leather, écru
  lace, white and gold and / or silver
  brocades, moire, a few pale printed
  fabrics, organza
2 yd / 1.80 m lightweight wadding /
  batting, 60 in / 150 cm wide
assorted sizes of glass beads, pearls,
  gold and silver sequins, braids and
  ribbons, mother of pearl and glass
  buttons
124 shishas (approx ¾ in / 20 mm in
  diameter) and approx 20 more in
  various shapes and sizes
DMC écru, pale grey, pale yellow
  embroidery stranded cotton
thick DMC coton à broder
silver and gold metallic threads
freezer paper

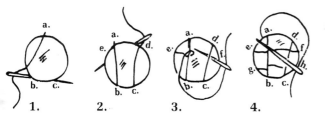

Shisha embroidery. *The use of small discs of mirror glass is a feature of the folk-embroidery of Northern and Western India. Sketches 1. to 4., above, show how to fix the fragment of mirror to the cloth. Sketches 5. to 8. show how a herringbone stitch is worked over the edge of the mirror, holding it firmly in place. I like to work the herringbone stitch fairly loose. To finish off, a row of chain stitch can be worked, close to the edge of the mirror (see the photograph of the sample for the border on page 96).*

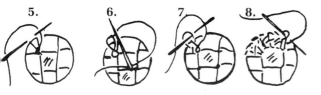

1. **Peacock panel.** Cut an oblong of cream-coloured silk dupion, 13 x 45 in / 33 x 115 cm. Stay-stitch the edges to prevent the silk from fraying. Enlarge peacock pattern on page 97, as instructed, once the right way up and once in reverse. Outline the peacock shapes lightly on the background silk, using a sharp hard pencil.

2. **Appliqueing the peacocks.** I used the freezer paper method, as outlined in 3. and 4. of the 'Kama' quilt on pages 75-76. Follow these instructions and applique the feet, the beak and the crown, then the body and finally the tail. Embroider the eye, the lines on the body and the feathers in the tail. Use beads for the crown.

3. **The elephant panel.** Cut an oblong of dupion silk 14 x 44 in / 36 x 112 cm. Enlarge the template on page 97, as instructed, to produce the 5 elephants. Start with the larger elephant and proceed as for the peacocks. Applique the trunk and head first (not the ear) and add the tusks and the head covers (there is a detail of one of the elephants on the title page of the book). Applique leg 1, with leg 2 overlapping it, then leg 3 and leg 4 (which has a bit of body and tail attached to it). Applique the blanket and lastly the ear and the howdah. Embroider the elephant's eye and its toes. Embroider anklets over its feet, add earrings and embroider the blanket and the howdah lavishly, using gold thread and picking out details with beads and sequins.

4. To finish both panels, cut wadding / batting to the same size, tack / baste together and work 'kantha' quilting (see page 96). Add some free-hand embroidery, beads and sequins.

5. **The central crazy patchwork panel.** Out of the foundation material, cut 2 17 in / 43 cm squares and 1 oblong 14 x 17 in / 36 x 43 cm for the top row; cut 2 oblongs 14 x 17 in / 36 x 43 cm and 1 20 x 17 in / 51 x 43 cm for the bottom row. Refer to instructions for crazy patchwork on page 113. Fill up each block and embellish it (see **General principles** on page 20 and paragraph 2. on page 90). Cut a piece of wadding / batting to the same size as each block. Tack / baste.

6. Square off the blocks so that their final measurements for the top row are 2 15 in / 38 cm squares and 1 12 x 15 in / 30½ x 38 cm; for the bottom row 2 12 x 15 in / 30½ x 38 cm and 1 18 x 15 in / 45½ x 38 cm. With right sides together oversew block 1. to block 2., and 2. to 3. Repeat for the second row and join both rows together. Embroider or couch ribbon or lace over the joins which will not be covered by the shisha strips (see 7. below).

7. **Strips of shisha embroidery.** Refer to the photograph of the peacock detail on page 93 and to the quilt on page 95. Cut 2 strips out of the foundation material, each measuring 5 x 44 in / 13 x 112 cm. Turn under 1 in / 25 mm on either side. The strip should now be 3 in / 75 mm wide. Press. Fold in

The finished quilt measures 64 x 47 in / 160 x 120 cm.

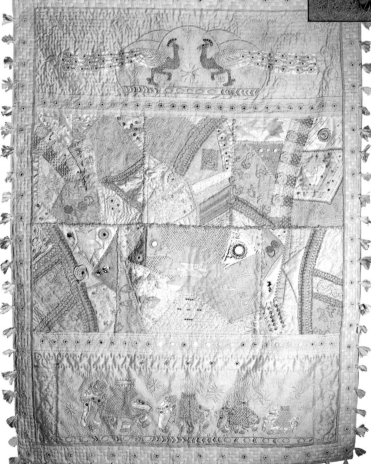

← *The peacock panel*

← *Strip of shisha embroidery*

← *The central crazy patchwork panel, made up of 6 blocks*

← *Strip of shisha embroidery*

← *The elephant panel*

← *The pieced border with tassels*

Above. A sample of 'kantha' quilting, which is a simple running stitch. It often accompanies simple motifs, worked in back stitch and satin stitch.

a.   **b.**

Above. The pieced border. Sample **a.** shows a 9-patch block, joined to the calico bars. In **b.**, is a calico square with the shisha in place, joined to the 3-patch bars. The seam allowances have been turned down to make these examples clearer.

half, wrong sides together, and press lightly. With a ruler and a sharp hard pencil, mark a line ¾ in / 2 cm either side of the centre fold (the marked area should be 1½ in / 4 cm wide). Find the middle of the long strip and, starting from that point, mark faint lines every 1½ in / 4 cm to give a total of 26 squares. With chain stitch or a machine-embroidery stitch go over all the lines, forming the squares. Draw 1 more line ⅜ in / 6 mm away from either edge of the strip. Work in chain stitch or in machine embroidery. Fix 1 shisha at the centre of each square (see shisha embroidery technique on page 94). Repeat for the 2nd strip. Slip-stitch over the joins, between the appliqued panels and the crazy patchwork central panel (refer to photograph of quilt on page 95).

8. **The border.** The mosaic-like border is made of patches of white habutai silk and of calico (the foundation fabric). Cut strips 1 in / 25 mm wide along the width of both fabrics. This includes a ¼ in / 6 mm seam allowance. Use a rotary cutter and a grid ruler. Join and machine-stitch 1 band of silk / calico strips as shown in **diagram 1.** and 1 as in **diagram 2.** Cut these vertically to the original width, i.e. 1 in / 25 mm. You now have 2 stacks of contrasting strips. Assemble alternate strips to obtain a 9-patch block. Cut a stack of calico bars, using **template a.** on page 97. Attach 1 bar to the top and bottom of the 9-patch block (see sample **a.** opposite). Cut 1 stack of calico squares, using **template b.** Attach 1 3-patch bar to the top and bottom of the square (see sample **b.** opposite). Attach the square to the block and repeat. To complete the borders, you will need 42 9-patch / bar blocks and 42 squares / 3-patch blocks for both long sides. For the top and bottom borders, you will need 30 9-patch and 30 square blocks. When the borders are complete, machine-stitch them to the quilt, ¼ in / 6 mm from the edge. Attach 1 shisha in the centre of each calico square (you may prefer to back the quilt before doing this).

9. Press the remainder of the white calico and cut an oblong to the exact size of the top of the quilt. Right sides together, machine-stitch ¼ in / 6 mm from the edge. Leave 1 16 in / 40 cm opening for turning the piece inside out. Slip-stitch the opening. Lay the quilt flat, tack / baste. Quilt 'in the ditch' (see instructions on page 121) along the blocks and the inner side of the border. Collect all your remaining scraps of fabric and cut them into strips ¼ in / 6 mm wide and 2¼ in / 55 mm long. Make little 'bundles' of 25 strips and turn into tassels. You'll need 58 tassels to go round 3 sides of the quilt (refer to the picture of the quilt).

Left. This sample shows drawn-thread embroidery worked on loosely woven mutka silk; a couple of round shishas, ready to be fixed, (although the circular ones appear most popular, shishas come in other shapes too); and a tassel made up of scraps of fabric, ready to be attached to the border.

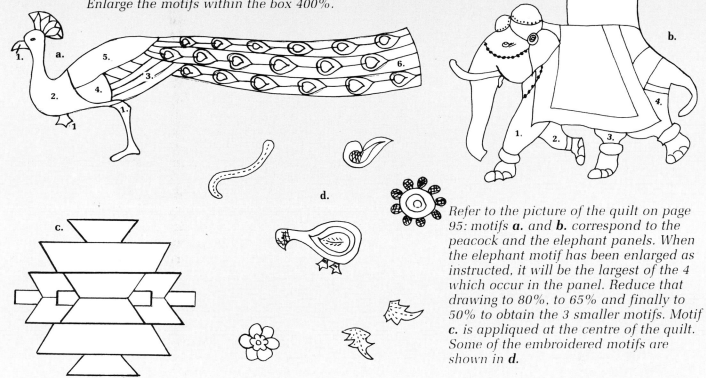

Enlarge the motifs within the box 400%.

a.

b.

c.

d.

Refer to the picture of the quilt on page 95: motifs **a.** and **b.** correspond to the peacock and the elephant panels. When the elephant motif has been enlarged as instructed, it will be the largest of the 4 which occur in the panel. Reduce that drawing to 80%, to 65% and finally to 50% to obtain the 3 smaller motifs. Motif **c.** is appliqued at the centre of the quilt. Some of the embroidered motifs are shown in **d.**

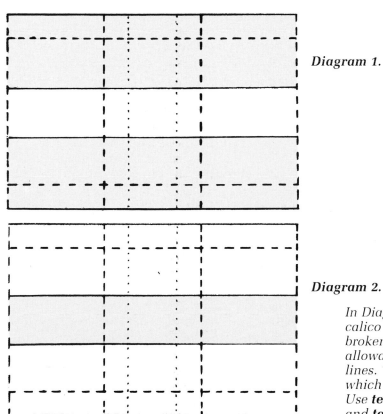

Diagram 1.

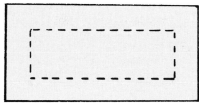

Template a.

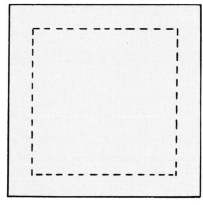

Template b.

Diagram 2.

In Diagrams **1.** and **2.**, the shaded areas represent the calico strips while the silk strips are shown in white. The broken horizontal lines show the remaining seam allowances. The vertical broken lines are the cutting lines. The dotted lines show the tiny finished squares which will form the pieced border (½ in / 13 mm square). Use **template a.** (shown life size) to cut the calico bars and **template b.** for the calico squares.

FAIRGROUND IMPRESSIONS

Jill Essery

SHOPPING LIST

1 yd / 90 cm cream-coloured felt
2 yd / 1.80 m gold lamé, 44 in / 112 cm
   wide
½ yd / 50 cm each of 4 different fabrics
   (silks or sateen) in blue, purple,
   yellow and mustard
½ yd / 25 cm each of 4 different fabrics,
   ranging from yellow to dark brown,
   including bronze lamé
1 yd / 90 cm dark brown gauze
1 yd / 90 cm black cotton fabric for the
   backing
1 yd / 90 cm lightweight wadding /
   batting
1 yd / 90 cm medium-weight wadding /
   batting
1 yd / 90 cm Stitch 'n' Tear backing
1 skein quilting wool
½ yd / 50 cm pelmet-weight Vilene
1 small piece of butter muslin
1 small piece of white cotton fabric
small quantity of toy stuffing
4¾ yd / 4.30 m No. 4 piping cord or
   decorative cord in similar width
7¾ yd / 7 m No. 2 piping cord or
   decorative cord in similar width
metallic machine-embroidery threads
cream-coloured sewing thread
beads, bugles and sequins to tone
   with fabrics
small curved needle
twin needle suitable for your sewing
   machine

This wallhanging forms part of a series inspired by old-fashioned fairground organs and carousels. It is worked in 2 sections and uses reverse applique and trapunto quilting which produces an interesting relief effect.

1. Out of the white felt cut 2 oblongs 18 x 20 in / 46 x 51 cm and 12 x 20 in / 30 x 51 cm respectively. Cut 2 pieces of gold lamé and 2 pieces of lightweight wadding / batting to the same sizes as the felt. Place the gold lamé pieces *under* their felt counterparts. Enlarge **diagrams 1.** and **2.** as instructed. Transfer the designs on to Stitch 'n' Tear backing and lay them over the cut pieces of felt, which will form the top and lower sections of the hanging respectively. Using the drawing for guidance, layer pieces of yellow, purple and blue fabrics under the relevant parts of the design (check with original diagrams) and pin into position. These pieces should be 1¼ in / 3 cm larger than the shape they are to fill and may overlap each other. In the *lower section* of the hanging, the piece of yellow fabric should be the same size as the felt. Place these various layers over the relevant piece of batting / wadding and tack / baste together.

2. **Upper section of the hanging.** Through the Stitch 'n' Tear backing, machine-stitch the main outlines of the scrolls and cartouches, using cream-coloured thread. Score the paper along the stitched lines with a needle, carefully lift out the pieces which were *inside* the shapes and keep them to one side. Leave the remaining Stitch 'n' Tear in place. With small, sharp-pointed scissors, cut the felt just inside the machine-stitched lines, revealing the gold lamé underneath. Reposition the paper pieces you saved before cutting out the felt, and use them as a guide to work the internal quilting lines on the scrolls and cartouches with gold thread (see photographic detail on page 100). Remove and discard paper from these areas only. Cut back the lamé in the appropriate places to reveal the coloured layers underneath. If the edges fray badly, go over them with a small zigzag stitch.
NOTE. It is easy to snip through more layers of fabric than you intended to cut away. Place 1 layer of medium-weight wadding / batting under the work, and machine-stitch around the hatched shapes, using cream-coloured thread. Remove the paper from these and cut away the felt and lamé to reveal the coloured fabrics underneath. Using cream-coloured thread, machine-quilt along the lines (dotted on diagram). Run your nail around all the cut-out shapes to raise any loose thread and trim off.

Opposite page. The finished hanging measures 26 x 20 in / 66 x 51 cm.

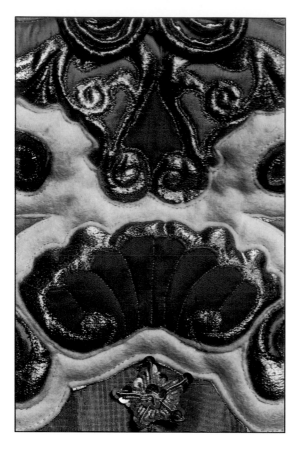

Above. A detail of the upper section of the hanging, showing the quilting.

Opposite page. Diagrams 1. and 2.
Enlarge both 300%. The diagrams have been coloured to guide you (see colour key below). The white areas represent the felt panel. In **diagram 2.** *do not yet trace the angel motif. It is shown here as a colour guide. Instructions for the motif are given in paragraph 8, and a special sketch is supplied on page 103.*

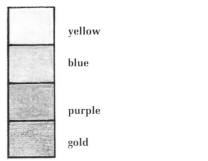

yellow

blue

purple

gold

3. Cut away, through *all layers*, along the inner cutting line (you end up with a 3-sided frame). Keep aside.

4. **Lower section of the hanging**. Repeat all steps described in 2. above. Leave the central section, where the cupids will eventually fit, covered in white felt.

5. **The organ pipes motif.** This sits centrally on the upper section of the hanging and consists of separate geometric shapes which fit over each other. Enlarge the **templates a.** to **f.** on pages 102-103 as instructed. Out of the pelmet-weight Vilene, cut 1 piece from templates **a.**, **b.**, **e.** and **f.**; and 2 from **c.** and **d.** Transfer the lines marked on the templates on to the *wrong* side of the relevant Vilene shapes (in the case of **c.** and **d.**, the 2nd shape of each pair must be reversed). The dotted lines on the templates indicate where the pieces will overlap. Cut the same shapes again out of lightweight wadding / batting. Use the templates to cut the coloured cloth to cover the Vilene pieces (refer to photograph of hanging for colour guidance). For **b.** I used gold lamé, covered with one layer of dark brown gauze. Allow an extra 1¼ in / 3 cm for turning over the top edge of the Vilene shapes. Pin the wadding / batting shapes, then the relevant fabric, face up, over the upper side of the Vilene pieces (the drawn lines appear on the wrong side). Machine-stitch from the *wrong* side along the drawn lines, making sure that the thread in the spool is the colour you wish to show on the right side of the work. Do this on **a.**, **b.**, **c.**, **d.** and **e.** On **b.** I then ran lines of zigzag stitchery on the right side of the piece; on **e.** satin-stitch bands, using the widest zigzag setting on the machine. Turn the fabric neatly over the top edge of each piece of Vilene and fix it at the back with a row of herringbone stitches.

6. On **f.**, position the fabric over the right side of the Vilene. Run a line of tacking / basting showing the eventual position of **e.** Hand-stitch the base of **e.** over **f.** using a waxed doubled thread. Run a line of tacking / basting, showing the eventual position of **d.** Fix **d.** and repeat these steps for **c.** and **a.** Bead the shapes to suggest the pipes of the organ, using a variety of bugles, beads and sequins and any other ornament. Finally catch the coloured shapes at strategic points with a few hand stitches.

7. **Positioning the organ pipe motif within the upper section of the hanging.** Centre the organ pipe motif behind the scrolled 'frame' you made at the beginning. The felt inner edges should overlap evenly all round. Pin in position. Attach the felt frame to the organ motif by running a line of machine stitches over the inner edge of the felt so that you finish with a ⅝ in / 2 cm wide felt surround on 3 sides of the brown / yellow organ motif (refer to picture of hanging). Trim back the excess felt, close to the stitching line. To finish off the base of the organ motif, cut a strip of dark brown fabric 9½ x 2 in / 24 x 5 cm. Fold it in half, lengthwise. Run a line of stitching, ½ in / 15 mm from the edge. Turn right side out

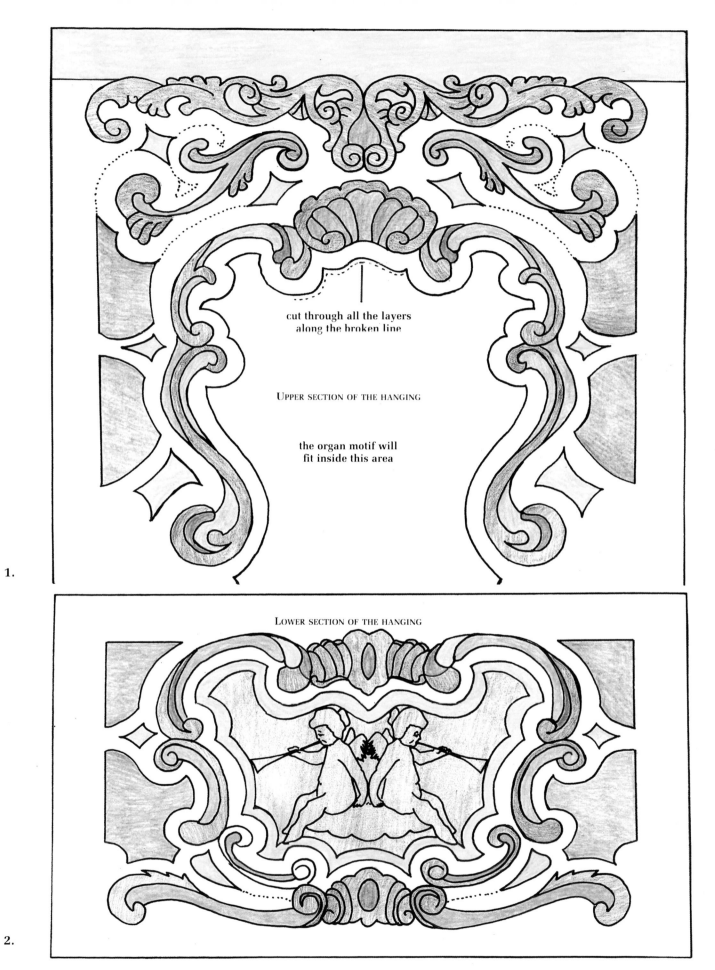

cut through all the layers
along the broken line

UPPER SECTION OF THE HANGING

the organ motif will
fit inside this area

1.

LOWER SECTION OF THE HANGING

2.

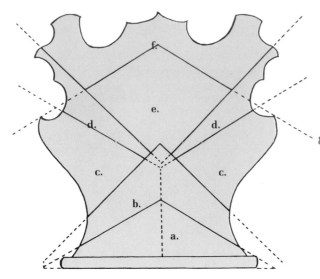

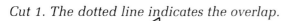

Enlarge the shapes on this page and the next 400%. The sketch above shows how the templates form the organ motif.

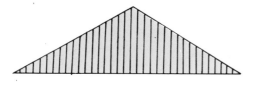

Template a. Cut 1.

Template b.

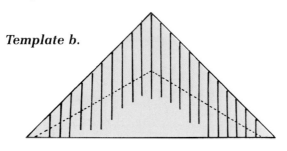

Cut 1. The dotted line indicates the overlap.

Template c.

Template d.

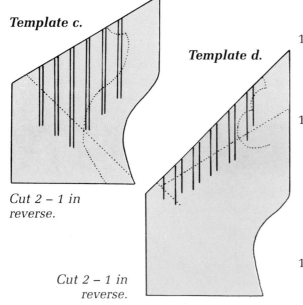

Cut 2 – 1 in reverse.

Cut 2 – 1 in reverse.

and stuff with quilting wool to form a rolled edge. Neaten the ends to leave a roll 8½ in / 22 cm long. Flatten the roll slightly and slip-stitch the top edge on to the base of the pipe motif. Leave the lower edge loose – it will be fixed *after* the upper and lower sections are joined.

8. **The lower section – the cupid motif.** This is worked in trapunto quilting (see page 122) and reverse applique and applied as a complete panel over the centre of the lower section. Enlarge the cupid design on page 103 as instructed and trace off on to Stitch 'n' Tear backing. Cut out the shape and lay it over a piece of gold lamé. Run a line of tacking / basting around the outer edge. Cut the cloth, allowing an extra 1½ in / 4 cm all round. Change the foot of the machine to do free-machine embroidery (see page 110, paragraph 6). Using this technique and dark metallic thread, machine-stitch the outlines. Tear off the paper. Place 2 layers of gauze over the lamé. Cut a piece of white cotton backing fabric 1 in / 25 mm larger all round than the cupid figures. Place it under them. Free-machining, go once more over the complete outlines of the figures, but *not* the hair, face or wing details, following the previous stitching lines through the gauze. Cut away the gauze from over the figures, exposing the lamé. If it threatens to fray, retrace the outlines with a close and narrow zigzag stitch. Trapunto-quilt the figures from the *wrong* side by cutting small slits into the cotton backing and pushing in toy stuffing to fill the bodies of the cupids. Fit the normal foot back on the machine.

9. Take the lower section of the hanging prepared in 1. above. Machine-stitch a contour line around the inner felt area, ½ in / 15 mm from the framing scrolls. Cut back the felt and the gold lamé layers to reveal the yellow silk underneath. Centre the cupid motif over the yellow area and machine-stitch over the line of tacking / basting to applique the motif. Trim off excess cloth, close to the stitched lines. Go over these lines again, using metallic thread and a narrow close zigzag stitch.

10. Out of the mustard-coloured fabric, cut 2 bias strips, each 21 x 2½ in / 53 x 6 cm. Use them to bind the top and bottom edges of the 2 sections of the panel. Roll the strip over to the back of the work and hand-stitch neatly on the wrong side.

11. **Joining the upper and lower sections of the hanging.** Overlap the bottom edge of the upper section over the top of the lower section by ½ in / 15 mm to join the 2 pieces. Trim off excess wadding / batting at the back and machine-stitch across, using cream-coloured thread and a small zigzag stitch. Keep the rolled strip at the base of the organ pipes clear. When the 2 sections are joined, slip-stitch the bottom edge of the rolled strip over the join.

12. **Gold columns at the side of the hanging.** The top part of these is worked in corded quilting, the bottom part in twin-needle stitching. For the corded quilting section, cut 2 strips

of pelmet-weight Vilene, 16 x 1¼ in / 41 x 3 cm and 2 strips of medium-weight wadding / batting, to the same length, but twice the width. Fold these in half. Cut 2 strips of gold lamé, 18 x 4 in / 46 x 10 cm and 2 of cotton backing fabric to the same size. Pin the backing fabric to the back of the lamé. Refer to instructions for corded quilting in para 7, page 34. Work diagonal lines across 1 column, reversing the direction of the lines for the one opposite. For the 2 sections worked in the twin-needle technique, cut 2 strips of pelmet-weight Vilene 10½ x 1¼ in / 27 x 3 cm and 2 of medium-weight wadding / batting to the same length, but twice the width. Fold these in half. Cut 2 strips of gold lamé, 12 x 4 in / 31 x 10 cm. Use 2 reels of cotton on the top of the machine, threading each through opposite sides of the tension wheel. Use a twin needle, suitable for your sewing machine. Stitch straight vertical lines, a machine-foot width apart. Place the folded-over wadding / batting on the corresponding strips of Vilene. Wrap the corresponding quilted lengths of gold lamé over this and fix it at the back with rows of herringbone stitch (this will be hidden). Tuck the ends of the lamé strips neatly under, ensuring that the lengths of the columns match the upper and lower sections of the hanging.

13. I used rouleau decorations on the sides and the top of the hanging to suggest mouldings. As an alternative, I have specified quantities of toning cord, in 2 thicknesses, in the shopping list. If you decide to use rouleau, refer to instructions on page 123. Use the specified piping cord and make up the specified quantities in both thicknesses. Refer to the picture of the hanging and twine the rouleaux or cords around the columns and across the top. Slip-stitch into place. Position the embellished columns over the sides of the hanging. Tack / baste firmly through all the layers. Attach the columns to the panel, using a waxed doubled thread and a curved needle.

14. Cut an oblong of cotton backing fabric, 31 x 22 in / 79 x 56 cm. Cut a strip of pelmet-weight Vilene 19 x 3 in / 48 x 8 cm. Machine-stitch on to the *wrong* side of the cotton backing, along the width of the fabric, 2½ in / 7 cm from the top of the backing fabric. Prepare 4 loops to fit the size of the pole and attach them at regular intervals over the Vilene-strengthened area. Cut 2 oblongs of medium-weight wadding / batting, ½ in / 15 mm smaller than the actual size of the hanging. Tack / baste to the back of the hanging. Pin the backing fabric over it, making sure the loops are correctly aligned. Turn in the edges and slip-stitch the backing neatly, close to the outer edges of the hanging.

Right. Enlarge this sketch 400% and refer to the instructions for trapunto quilting on page 122.

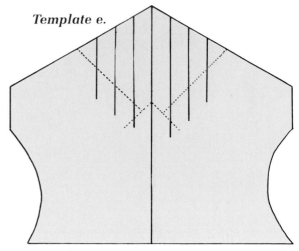

Template e.

Cut 1.

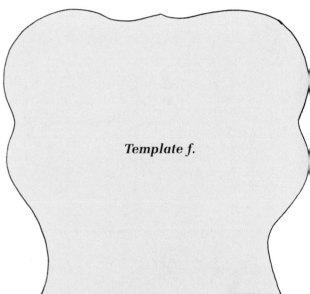

Template f.

*Cut 1. This template forms the background of the whole motif. The other templates overlap each other on top of **f**. Refer to the picture of the hanging on page 99.*

BEDSPREAD & MATCHING DAY PILLOW

Gilly Wraight

SHOPPING LIST

quantities given are sufficient for both
the bedspread and the cushion
½ yd / 45 cm habutai silk,
45 in / 112 cm wide
1½ yd / 1.40 m pink cotton fabric,
47 in / 120 cm wide
1 yd / 90 cm blue cotton fabric,
47 in / 120 cm wide
62 toning wooden beads, ¼ in / 6 mm
in diameter
4 yd / 3.60 m each of deep blue, pale
blue, deep pink, pale pink narrow
ribbon (these quantities are nominal)
1½ yd / 1.40 m blue cord *and*
2 matching tasels (optional)
1 yd / 90 cm soft lightweight wadding /
batting
cotton bed cover *or* corresponding
quantity of plain furnishing fabric:
3 x 2½ yd / 2.70 x 2.30 m
1 18 x 28 in / 46 x 71 cm cushion pad
1 skein of thick blue embroidery thread
matching blue and pink sewing threads
toning machine-embroidery threads
invisible nylon thread
quilting pencil
2 pots of silk dye in pink and blue (no
steam-fixing)
1 sponge brush
4 small dishes for the dye and clean
water

Enlarge this template 400%.

Template 1.

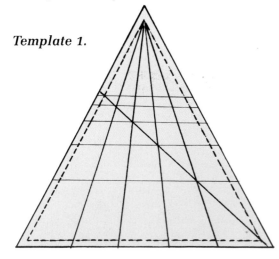

I chose soft romantic colours to work this unusual bedspread and its matching decorative pillow. On page 81 you will find a small wallhanging in which I have already used the pyramidal design, combined with beading and hand-dyed Suffolk puffs. Work 1 of these projects to add to an existing decor, or work all 3 to produce a complete look.

1. **The bedspread**. For the central motif of blue and pink pyramids, enlarge **template 1.** opposite, as instructed. Make a master out of cardboard and use it to cut 6 pyramids out of the blue fabric, and 3 of the pink. Transfer the internal lines on to the blue pyramids only. Using blue machine-embroidery thread, run 1 row of stitches over the internal lines within each pyramid, *including the diagonal*. Run over these lines again – *except the diagonal* – 4 times, alternating the blue and pink machine-embroidery threads. Allow the threads to hang loose at the edges – see sample pyramid on page 106. Run your fingernail over each row of stitches before doing the next to avoid excessive puckering. Press.

2. Take the original tracing of the template again and remove the seam allowance. Centre it over the *wrong* side of one of the pyramids. Trace its outline with the quilting pencil. This will give an accurate sewing line when you join the pyramids together. Repeat for all pyramids, including the 3 pink ones. Refer to the picture of the bedspread – the 9 blue and pink triangles are assembled to form a large pyramid. Pin and machine-stitch to each other the 5 triangles which form the base of the pyramid. Join the 3 which form the 2nd row. Join these 2 rows together and add the final blue triangle which is the top of the pyramid. Press seams.

3. Place the pyramid face down on a table. Turn down the raw outer edges and tack / baste them. Press. Using the finished pyramid as a template, cut the wadding / batting a little smaller than the finished pyramid. Remove the tacking / basting from the edges of the pyramid and insert the piece of wadding / batting, trimming it slightly to fit, if necessary. Tack / baste these 2 layers together.

4. **Appliqueing the pyramid on to the bedspread**. Measure 28½ in / 71 cm from the bottom of the bedspread. Mark with a pin. The base of the pyramid will rest on that line. Measure the width of the base of the pyramid and the width of the bedspread and centre the pyramid over it. Tack / baste

104

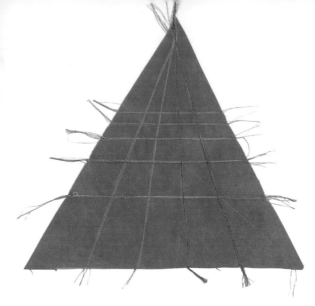

A pyramid with the completed machine embroidery.

in position. Hand-applique or machine-top-stitch (stronger), close to the edge. The individual triangles can be quilted 'in the ditch'.

5. Place the bedspread over a large table. Pin lengths of narrow ribbon, using the diagonal lines in the blue triangles of the pyramid as a guide. Trail them over the pyramid and down 1 side of the bedspread, alternating the colours. If you decide to go right across the bedspread, you will need to increase the quantities given in the shopping list. You could also tie little bows out of the ribbon. It is all a question of taste. Apply the ribbon with a straight or zigzag stitch, using the invisible thread. You could couch the ribbon by hand, using toning embroidery thread, if you prefer.

6. **Dyeing the silk for the Suffolk puffs**. Pour a small amount of blue dye in one of the dishes, dilute with a little water and repeat for the pink dye. The 3rd dish is for mixing the colours. Have clean water ready too. Cut a small piece of silk habutai to practise on. Tape it and the remainder of the silk to sheets of paper. Using the sponge brush, dampen the silk sparingly with clean water. Experiment with the dyes on the small piece of silk first until you are satisfied with the shades of pink and blue. The sponge brush can be rinsed off quickly between colour applications and dried with kitchen paper. Allow the fabric to dry. Fix according to the manufacturer's instructions.

7. **The Suffolk puffs**. Refer to instructions given in paragraph 8., page 80, but use the following circle sizes and quantities: cut 1 circle 8½ in / 21 cm, 1 7½ in / 19 cm, 3 6 in / 15 cm, 2 5 in / 13 cm, 3 4½ in / 11 cm, 1 3½ in / 9 cm, 4 3 in / 7 cm in diameter. Make up the puffs and pin them over the pyramid, moving towards the top of the bedspread. This is best done on the bed itself, making sure the design will not be hidden by the pillow. Applique them with a few stitches. Distribute the beads among the puffs. Sew them on securely, using strong embroidery thread.

This sketch shows the construction of the top of the pillow. The broken lines on the pink surround indicate the position of the top-stitching (see paragraph 13, page 107).

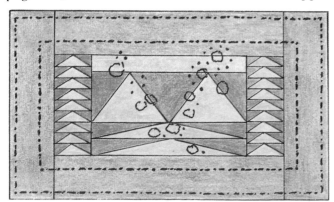

The pillow. It has an inset panel made up of American seamed patchwork and incorporates the pyramid motif and 2 strips worked in the popular 'flying geese' pattern. See sketch opposite.

8. Refer to 1. above and, using the cardboard template (complete with seam allowance), cut 2 blue and 2 pink pyramids. Cut 1 of the pink pyramids in half lengthwise. Machine-embroider the blue triangles as in 1. above. Assemble with the pink one. Join the half pink triangles at either end of the strip. Press. Enlarge **templates 2.-6.** on page 107, as instructed.

9. Use **template 2.** and cut 1 shape out of a *folded* piece of blue fabric. Join onto the top of the pink / blue pyramids. Place **template 3.** over a piece of blue folded fabric and cut 2 shapes. Using **template 4.**, cut

4 pink shapes (2 should be in reverse if the chosen fabric has a 'wrong' side). Following instructions for American seamed patchwork on page 114, assemble the pink and blue shapes. Press. Attach this section to the base of the pyramid panel.

10. **Flying-geese strips**. Enlarge **templates 5.** and **6.** Use **template 5.** to cut 18 blue triangles. Use **template 6.** to cut 36 pink triangles. Refer to American seamed patchwork on page 114 and make 2 strips with 9 blue triangles in each. Attach to either side of the pyramid panel. Press.

11. **Pink surround**. Measure 1 of the long dimensions of the oblong you have produced and cut 2 strips of pink fabric to the same length and 6¼ in / 16 cm wide. Pin to the top and bottom of the panel, right sides together. Machine-stitch. Press seams. Measure the length of 1 of the opposite sides. Cut 2 strips of pink fabric to that length and 6¼ in / 16 cm wide. Join as before. Press. The front of the pillow is now complete.

12. **Backing the pillow**. Measure the shorter dimension of the front of the cushion, cut 2 oblongs of pink fabric to that length, 27½ in / 70 cm and 15½ in / 40 cm wide respectively. Work a ⅔ in / 20 mm wide hem along 1 short dimension of each piece. Place the 2 oblongs, right sides together, over the front section of the pillow, allowing the excess fabric to overlap towards the centre of the pillow. Machine-stitch all round the pillow, ⅝ in / 15 mm from the edge. Turn pillow right side out. You can add a few press fasteners, or a piece of Velcro tape along the back opening to close it, if you wish. Press.

13. Place pillow case face up on the table. With a quilting pencil, mark a line ⅝ in / 15 mm all around from the outer edge of the pillow case. Top-stitch, using pink thread. Place pillow case face up on the table once more. Measure 3¾ in / 95 mm from the outer edges of the pillow case. With a ruler and a quilting pencil, outline this inner rectangle which will contain the cushion pad. Run a line of tacking / basting. Top-stitch with pink thread.

14. Apply lengths of narrow ribbon as explained in 5. above. Out of the remaining dyed habutai silk, cut 5 circles 4 in / 10 cm in diameter and 5 3 in / 8 cm. Make up into Suffolk puffs as in 7. above. Attach them to the pillow as desired. Stitch on a few beads. Attach lengths of blue cord and tassels, if desired (refer to picture of the pillow). Insert the pad.

Right. *Enlarge these 5 templates 400%.*

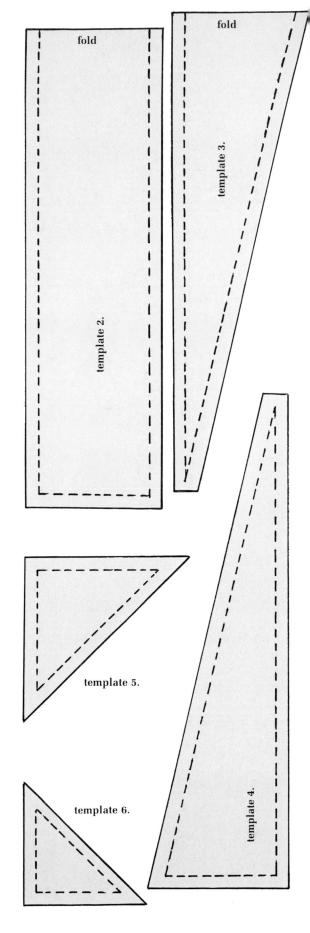

TREASURE BOX

Christine Donaldson

W hat will you store in this lovely casket? Jewellery, love letters? It was inspired by the work of the medieval goldsmiths who produced wonderful containers to be used as reliquaries or jewel chests. I made this one out of thick card covered in fabric, embellished with reverse appliqué, stencilling, machine-quilting and embroidering, not to mention 'precious' stones, sequins and beads.

The box is made from the base up and you should complete each section before measuring and cutting the next piece. This is because the thickness of the fabric can vary and therefore affect the final size of the covered card. This makes it impossible to give predetermined measurements or to cut out all the pieces at once. The final result depends on the board being cut accurately. Use a protractor or set-square to ensure that the pieces are square and true.

1. Cut 1 piece of *thick* card 5 x 9 in / 127 x 228 mm. It will form the bottom of the box. Cut 1 piece of *thin* card to the same size. It will form the base of the lining of the box. Pad 1 side of the *thick* card with felt, sticking it in place with a small amount of PVA adhesive. Trim the felt to the exact measurements of the base of the box. Keep the oblong of thin card to one side.

2. Out of the main fabric, cut a piece 8 x 12 in / 203 x 304 mm. Place over the felt-covered side of the base of the box, right side up. Pin in position, sticking the pins into the thickness of the board. Lace over the edges of the card and mitre the corners (see **diagram 1**).

3. The sides of the box are made from the *thick* card and are 3 in / 76 mm high. To measure the length of the short sides, lay the covered base of the box on a piece of *thick* card and mark the width of the base. Repeat for the 2nd short side. The long sides of the box are the length of the covered base, plus 2 thicknesses of thick card. This is to allow the long sides to butt over the ends of the short ones, giving neat, strong corners. Cut the lip of the lid out of *thick* card, ensuring that it is exactly the same length as the sides of the box. The height of the lip is ¾ in / 19 mm.

4. Cut out pieces of the main fabric to cover the sides of the box. They should be 1½ in / 38 mm larger all round than the cardboard pieces.

SHOPPING LIST

¾ yd / 70 cm of silk or fancy synthetic fabric, 36 in / 90 cm wide (main fabric)
½ yd / 45 cm contrasting silk dupion, 36 in / 90 cm wide (lining)
scraps of brightly coloured silks, metallic and fancy fabrics
1 yd / 90 cm butter muslin, 36 in / 90 cm wide
½ yd / 45 cm of felt, 36 in / 90 cm wide for padding
½ yd / 45 cm medium-weight polyester wadding / batting
strong thread or crochet cotton
1½ yd / 1.30 m thin gold cord
metallic machine-embroidery threads
sew-on paste jewels, sequins and beads
toning sewing polyester thread
curved needle
7-8 in / 177-203 mm diameter embroidery hoop
23 x 32 in / 59 x 81 cm mounting board / mill board
23 x 16 in / 59 x 41 cm firm but thin card
12 in / 30 cm square of oiled manilla paper or acetate for stencils
1 pot each of bronze and gold permanent fabric paint
Stanley knife or scalpel to cut card

Diagram 1.

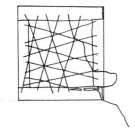
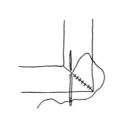

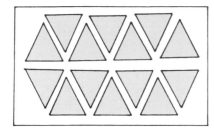

Diagram 2. Enlarge 200%. This is the design for the reverse applique.

Previous page. The finished box measures 9¼ x 5¼ in / 235 x 133 mm (6½ in / 140 mm in height).

Diagram 3. Enlarge 200%. This is the template for the stencil used on the long sides of the box.

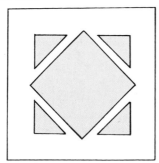

Diagram 4. Ladder stitch. The stitch between the folds is at right angles to the fabric and becomes invisible when pulled tight.

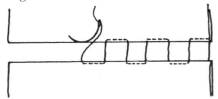

5. **Reverse applique patterns on the short sides of the box.** Using **diagram 2.**, transfer the pattern of triangles to the 2 smaller pieces of fabric; select 4 similarly sized scraps of brightly coloured silk or metallic fabric and lay them on top of each other with the main fabric on top, right side up. Pin and tack / baste together. Make a note of the order in which you laid the fabrics and also decide the colour scheme of the final triangles before you proceed to the next step. Machine-stitch around each triangle with a medium-length straight stitch. Using very sharp embroidery scissors, cut carefully through the top layer of the triangle, inside the line of stitching, down to the colour you wish to expose. Proceed with care – it is easy to snip through 2 layers of fabric by mistake and spoil the work. When all the triangles are complete, run a row of satin stitch around each one to finish off the edges and prevent fraying. Cut away the excess fabric at the back of the work to reduce bulk. Repeat for 2nd short side of the box.

6. **Free-machine embroidering the short sides of the box.** Before starting to embroider, stretch the piece of fabric tightly over a hoop. In this case, as the individual pieces are too small for the hoop, tack / baste each one on to a piece of muslin large enough to fit comfortably inside the hoop. Remove the foot of the machine. With the feed-dogs of the sewing machine lowered or covered (this depends on the make of the machine – check the manual) and using metallic embroidery thread, embroider a random straight stitch all around the reverse applique patterns – practise on a scrap of fabric first! Refer to the photograph of the box. Raise the feed-dogs again and work a row of satin stitch over the wavy line which encircles the group of appliqued triangles. Fix sequins and 'jewels' among the embroidery. Repeat for the other short side of the box.

7. **The long sides of the box.** Enlarge **diagram 3.** and make a stencil. Apply the stencil on to the pre-cut pieces of fabric, using the bronze-coloured paint. Allow it to dry and touch up the design lightly, using gold paint. Fix the colour according to the manufacturer's instructions. Support the fabric with a piece of muslin as before, but adding a piece of wadding / batting between the top fabric and the muslin. Tack / baste together and quilt, working a straight stitch around each stencilled shape, using gold embroidery thread. Cut away the excess wadding / batting. Embroider as in 6. above. Finish with a line of satin stitch. Sew on sequins and 'jewels'. Pin the embroidered fabric pieces over their respective pieces of card and lace firmly as before.

8. **Assembling the box.** Join 1 short side to a long one by hand, using a ladder stitch (see **diagram 4.**) and a small curved needle. Repeat for the next 2 sides. Join together to close the box, which should fit neatly over the base. Ladder-stitch together. Couch thin gold braid over the corner joins. (This braid must be very thin or it will interfere with the fit of the lid.)

9. **Lining the base of the box.** The box has an inner membrane, made out of the thin card and covered with silk dupion. Take the pre-cut oblong of *thin* card (see paragraph 1.) Fix wadding / batting over it with adhesive as before. Cut the lining fabric with 1½ in / 38 mm allowance all round. Wrap over the padded side and check the size inside the box. Trim the card slightly if necessary. Mitre the corners of the fabric. Lace as before. Drop the lined base inside the box.

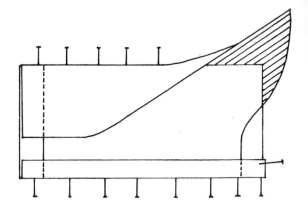

Diagram 5. Folding down and stitching the sides of the lining.

10. The inner side panels are made of *thick* card as they have to protrude above the sides of the box and support the lid. The height of the inner panels is 3¼ in / 95 mm. Take the inner measurements of the box. Cut out the board pieces and place all 4 side by side lengthwise over the lining fabric. Add 1½ in / 38 mm seam allowance at either side and at the base of the inner panels, but add 2½ in / 63 mm to what will be the top of the inner panel of the box. Fix wadding / batting over the card pieces. Lay the 1st long side, wadding / batting side down, over the wrong side of the fabric. Pin into the thickness of the card to hold the fabric in position, making the top turning 2¼ in / 55 mm wide. Lay the 1st short side against the long one, then follow with the remaining 2 panels. The corners should not be mitred, but folded and stitched as shown in **diagram 5**. Check the fit once more, then lace the fabric on to the card, ladder-stitching the 2 ends together. Drop the resulting inner membrane inside the box and ladder-stitch to the top edge of the box.

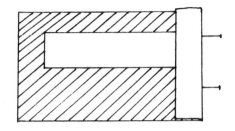

Diagram 6. Card for the lip of the lid pinned in position. The ends of the cloth should be turned over the card – not mitred.

11. **The lip of the lid.** Using the pre-cut card (see paragraph 3.) as a template, cut pieces out of the main fabric to cover the lip, allowing an extra 1½ in / 38 mm on 3 sides but 2½ in / 63 mm on 1 long side. Put each piece over a muslin base and machine-embroider as before. Cover the pieces of card with felt. Pin and stitch the embroidered fabric on to them, as shown in **diagrams 6.** and **6a.** Ladder-stitch the lip pieces together at the corners, checking that the lip fits neatly over the base of the box.

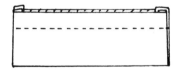

Diagram 6a. The fabric has been folded to enclose the card. A row of back stitch forms the seam (broken line on diagram). Ladder-stitch the ends.

12. **The triangular sides of the lid.** Measure the short ends of the lip which will give the size of the base of the triangles. The height from base to apex of the triangular pieces is 2½ in / 63 mm. Cut out 2 pieces of *thick* card. Use these as a template and trace this shape on to the main fabric with a quilting pencil. Cut, allowing for an extra 1½ in / 38 mm all round. Use the pattern in **diagram 7.** and stencil the shape over the cloth with bronze and gold paint, as before. Quilt and embroider as described in paragraph 7. Lace on to the card pieces.

Diagram 7. Enlarge 200%. This is the template for the stencil used on the triangular sides of the lid.

13. **The front and back panels of the lid.** Measure the long dimension of the lid lip and the side of the triangular lid section. Cut 2 pieces of *thick* card to this size, adding 1½ in / 38 mm seam allowance all around. Use the stencil which you made for the sides of the box as a template to mark the reverse applique pattern on the box lid. Proceed as in paragraph 5. Machine-embroider as before and add sequins

and 'jewels'. Pin into place, mitre corners and lace over the card pieces. Ladder-stitch the lid sides to the ends, then the lip to the base of the lid. Couch the gold cord along the joins of the lid top and sides. Sew beads firmly to either end of the lid.

14. Measure the inside dimensions of the lid (do not include the lip) and cut out of *thin* card. Cover with wadding / batting. Cover the lining fabric as before. Mitre the corners and lace. Ladder-stitch the pieces together. Place inside the box and ladder-stitch around the inner edge of the lid.

Below. *A detail from the centre of the quilt, 'Indian Reflections', by Gisela Thwaites (see page 93).*

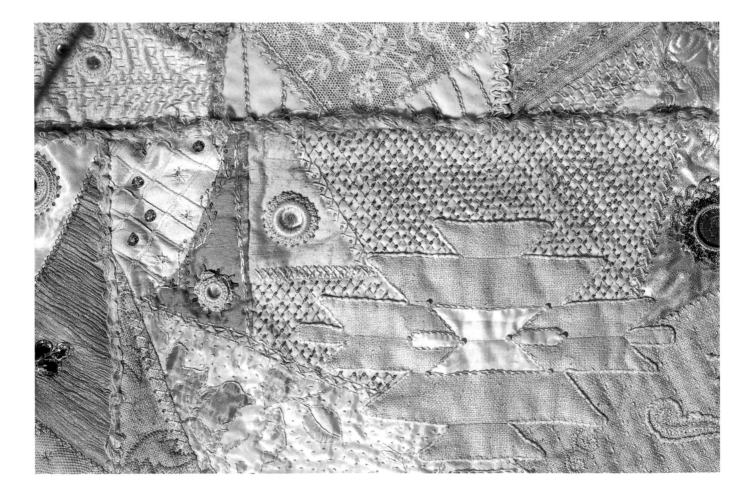

PATCHWORK TECHNIQUES

Crazy Patchwork

Crazy patchwork uses random pieces. It is now frequently made on the machine. In this case, the patches must have straight, *not* curved edges. It is worked on a piece of backing fabric.

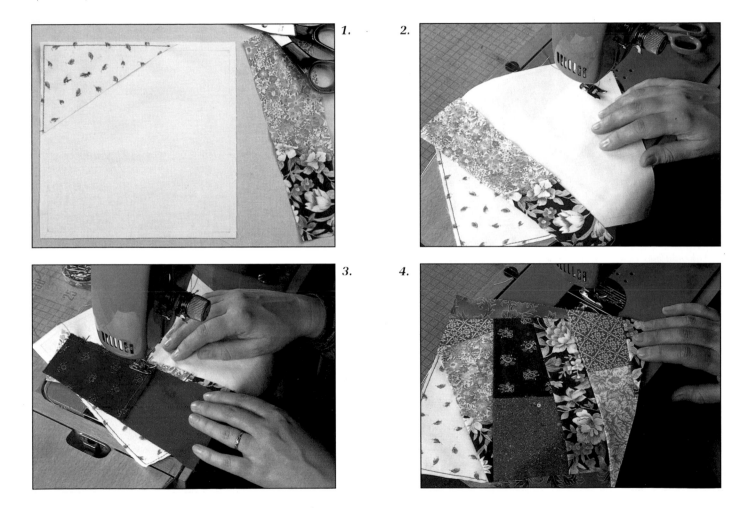

1. *Apply the 1st patch in a corner of the base fabric. Machine-stitch as shown.*

2. *You see 2 patches joined together, being added as a single piece.*

3. *Joining another unit. Do not trim off the ends. Cover the whole piece first.*

4. *Finished piece with edges trimmed off. Crazy patchwork was used in all the projects by Gisela Thwaites.*

English Patchwork

Cut paper templates to the exact size of the finished patch. The cloth is cut, leaving a ¼ in / 6 mm seam allowance all round. The patchwork is oversewn by hand, right sides together with tiny stitches which should not come through the paper. The patchwork is pressed with the paper templates still in place and these are removed only when the piece is ready for mounting.

1.

2.

3.

1. Master template, prepared patches tacked / basted on to their paper templates and 2 patches being stitched, working from right to left. It is important to catch only a couple of threads on each side.

2. Finished patches with the tacking / basting still on. The stitches should hardly show at all on the right side.

3. The back of the work after pressing. The purse illustrated on page 73 was made of English patchwork.

American Seamed Patchwork

1.

2.

3.

1. *Using the width of the presser foot as a guideline for the seams, join 3 pieces to form a complete unit.*

2. *A finished unit. Complete as many as you need, finger-press, then join the units together.*

3. *A finished length. This pattern is known as 'flying geese'. It was used in the pillow on page 105.*

Folded Star

The folded star was used on the wallhanging on page 15. The work is done on a piece of backing **fabric**, marked as shown below.

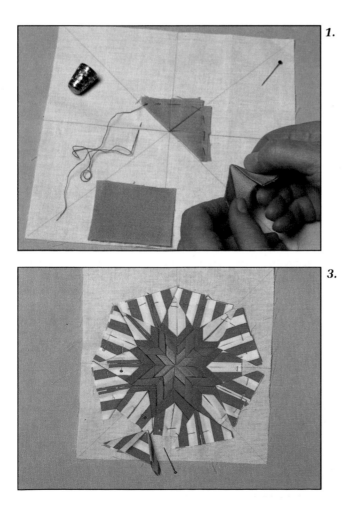

1.

2.

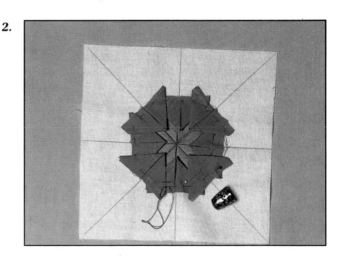

3.

1. *Fold / press 4 rectangles to form triangles, as shown. These form the centre of the star. NOTE that the fold at the centre of the triangles must sit over the lines drawn on the cloth. Accuracy is vital to the success of this piece.*

2. *The 1st row of 8 triangles being pinned and stitched in position.*

3. *The star is almost complete. Finally, the point of each triangle must be caught with an invisible stitch.*

Seminole Patchwork

This clever technique was developed by the Seminole tribe in America when they were first introduced to the sewing machine. It can be used to produce a variety of geometric shapes. It was used for the chessboard on page 26 and in the wallhanging on page 15.

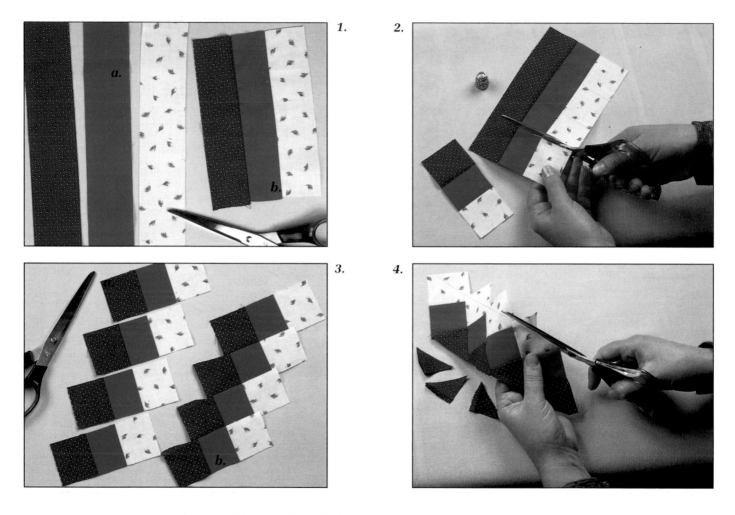

1. *Cut 3 strips as in **a.**, then machine-stitch as in **b.***

2. *Draw lines at right angles across the sewn strips. The spacing is equal to the width of the original strips. Cut.*

3. ***a.** Re-align pieces. Machine-stitch as in **b.***

4. *Draw a line on either side of the diamonds, leaving ¼ in / 6 mm seam allowance, and cut as shown. The strip is now ready.*

Log Cabin

Log cabin consists of narrow strips arranged around a centre square. The pieces are fixed on to a patch of white fabric on which the sewing lines have been marked. Remember to work clockwise. Normally, half of the block is worked in light fabrics and the other half in dark.

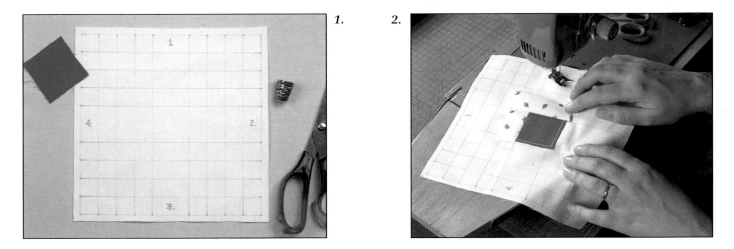

1. *The backing fabric has been marked with a fabric marker. The centre square goes on first, followed by the 1st strip.*

2. *The 1st strip has been finger-pressed and the 2nd has been added. The latter has been turned down and the work is ready for the 3rd strip.*

Log Cabin (Pineapple Variation)

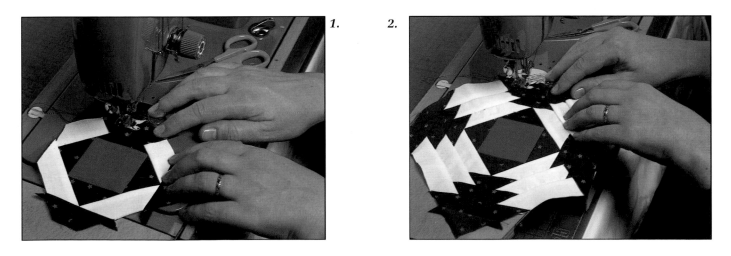

1. *The pineapple variation does not use a backing fabric. The pieces go on clockwise round the central square. The seams are pressed away from the centre.*

2. *The block is almost complete. This form of log cabin was used in the wallhanging on page 15.*

Japanese Folded Patchwork

Two versions of this work are shown in the book. The one described below appears in the wallhanging on page 15. Another version is used in the bag on page 65. The 1st step illustrated below is common to both versions.

1.

2.

3.

1. *Cut circles of cloth and cardboard templates to the size given in the projects. Run a line of gathers close to the edge of the cloth. Fit over the ironing template and pull the thread taut. Press and allow to cool before removing the template.*

2. *Machine-stitch 2 contrasting squares. Repeat and join the 2 strips to form a square. Press.*

3. *Place square over a piece of wadding / batting (same size). Turn down the edges of the circle, as shown. Pin in position. Quilt, using coton perlé.*

Cathedral Window

This method was used to produce the bag on page 87. It combines machine- and hand-sewing.

1.

2.

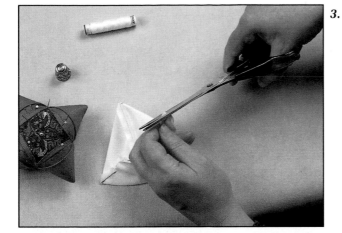 **3.**

4.

5.

6.

7.

1. Cut the basic square (size given in project). Fold it in half, machine-stitch down 1 side, then repeat for the other, as shown.

2. Press seam open and trim corners. Repeat. Fold pocket across to form a square. Pin the open side, as shown.

3. Machine-stitch 2nd seam, leaving small gap. Press seam, trim corners.

4. The square has been turned out and the small gap closed with slip stitches.

5. Bring 2 of the corners towards the centre and anchor-stitch (seams uppermost).

6. Join 2 shapes along folded sides, oversew.

7. Pin coloured centres (cut, using the template provided with project), turn down the plain coloured edges over the square. Hem-stitch neatly.

Secret Garden

This is a variation of Cathedral Window. It was used in the quilt on page 91.

1. **a.** Cut a square to the size given in the project; **b.** turn down the seam allowance; **c.** turn down the 1st corner as shown and repeat for the other 3 to produce a small square; **d.** cut the middle square to the size given in the project.

1. **2.**

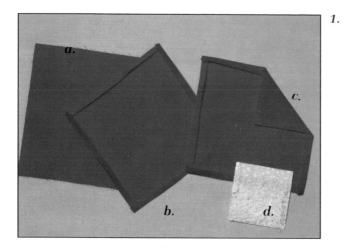
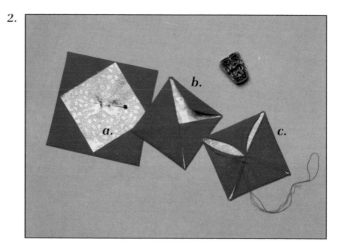

2. **a.** Lay the printed square over the plain, as shown; **b.** fold the corners down over the squares; **c.** hem-stitch the edges neatly.

Machine Applique

1. Fusible material being ironed on to the wrong side of the fabric.

2. Cut accurately around the drawn shape and remove the paper backing.

1. **2.**

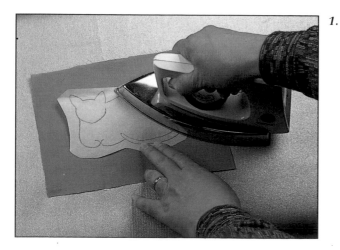
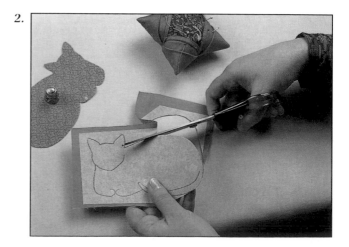

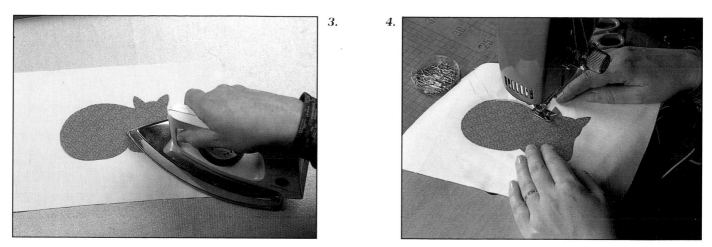

3. Place shape, adhesive side down, over the base fabric and press as shown.

4. Satin-stitch around the edges as shown. Details such as the cat features are then worked by hand in stem stitch.

Quilting

The original purpose of quilting was to hold several layers of fabric together to produce a warm covering. The technique can be used to produce designs of amazing complexity and beauty.

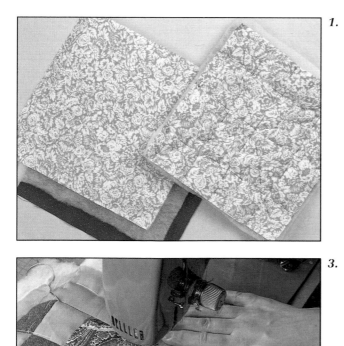

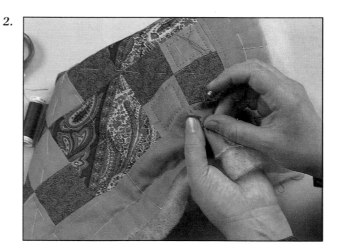

1. Tack / baste the back of the quilt, the wadding / batting and the top of the quilt.

2. Hand-quilting, away from the seam. If you need a guideline, use a pale quilting pencil or tailor's chalk, tracing as you go along.

3. Quilting 'in the ditch', i.e. into the seam line. It can of course also be done by hand.

Trapunto Quilting

Trapunto quilting is used to produce high-relief motifs such as the cupids in the wallhanging on page 99.

1. *Trace the motif over the cloth which is placed over a piece of cotton backing material. Machine-stitch along the marked outline.*

2. *Make a small slit at the back of the motif and insert a small amount of quilting wool. Close the slit with a few herringbone stitches. The example on the table shows the completed relief motif.*

1.   **2.**

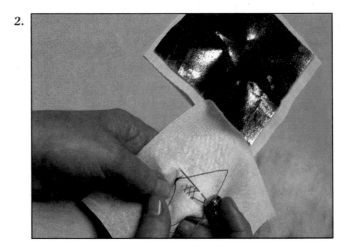

Binding & Mitring

The traditional way of finishing off a quilt. The golden rule is to use a strip 6 times the finished width of the bound edge.

1. *Cut the strip on the straight grain of the cloth and fold over as shown.*

2. *Starting from the centre of 1 side and working on the upper side of the quilt, machine-stitch up to the seam allowance. Fold the strip along the diagonal, as shown.*

1.   **2.**

3.

4.

3. *Fold corner, as shown. Machine-stitch down the 2nd side.*

4. *Back of the quilt. Fold the strip over and slip-stitch, mitring the corner as shown.*

Making Rouleau

1. *Fit a zipper or a piping foot on the machine. Cut a bias strip. Machine-stitch to encase a length of piping cord. NOTE that the cord should be twice the length of rouleau you want to produce. Start sewing in the middle of the cord, attaching the end of the bias strip firmly to the cord (see **a.**).*

2. *The fingers of the left hand are placed over the bias strip, while the other hand pulls gently and evenly at the end where sewing started (**a.**), allowing the finished rouleau to appear. A length of it is shown coiled on the right-hand side.*

1.

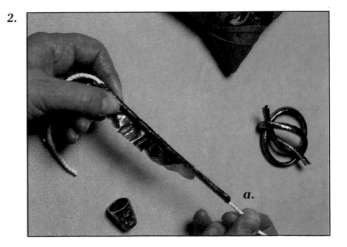
2.

Piping Around a Cushion

This technique provides an elegant and professional finish to a cushion. (See page 47 for instance.)

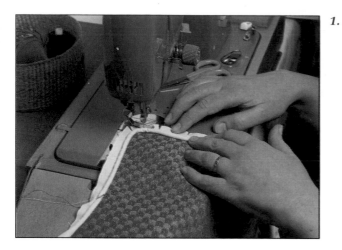

1.

1. *Fit a piping or a zipper foot on the sewing machine (consult your manual). Cut a bias strip. Insert the piping cord and machine-stitch as close as possible to the cord (you should start sewing at the centre of 1 side, as shown). Clip the bias strip as it goes round the corner. It looks better if the piping curves round the corner, rather than being applied at right angles.*

Tassels

These, large or small, appear with most of Christine Donaldson's projects.

1. *2.*

1. *Wrap the yarn over a piece of card, as shown. Tie the 'bundle' at one end. Cut the other at the edge of the card.*

2. *Wrap yarn around the top of the tassel to form the head. Finish it off neatly with a needle, losing the stitches among the yarn. Trim off the loose ends of the tassel. A finished example can be seen on the left of the picture.*

LIST OF SUPPLIERS

United Kingdom

John Lewis plc, Oxford Street, London W1A 1EX (general fabrics and haberdashery)
Liberty plc, Regent Street, London W1R 6AH (fine fabrics and haberdashery)
Harrods Ltd, Knightsbridge, London SW1X 7XL (fine fabrics and haberdashery)
Pongees Ltd, 184-186 Old Street, London EC1V 9FR (silk fabrics – mostly plain)
Borovick Fabrics Ltd, 16 Berwick Street, London W1V 4HP (exotic fabrics)
The Thai Silk Shop in Tenterden, 104 High Street, Tenterden, Kent TN30 6IIT (silk fabrics – small amounts suitable for patchwork)
Strawberry Fayre, Chagford, Devon TQ13 8EN, mail order only (cotton fabrics – special 'Amish' range)
The Country Store, 68 Westbourne Road, Marsh, Huddersfield, W. Yorkshire, also mail order
Crimple Craft, 1 Freemans Way, Forest Lane, Wetherby Road, Harrogate, Yorkshire HG3 1RW, also mail order (American and English cotton fabrics)
Piecemakers, 13 Manor Green Road, Epsom, Surrey KT19 8RA, also mail order (large range of fabrics)
The Quilt Room, 20 West Street, Dorking, Surrey RH4 1BL, also mail order (fabric – quilting supplies)
George Weil & Sons, The Warehouse, Reading Arch Road, Redhill, Surrey RH1 1HG (fabric paints and dyes – silks etc prepared for dyes and paint)
Quilters Haven, 68 High Street, Wickham Market, Suffolk IP13 0QU (quilting supplies, fabrics)
Dashca, Burwash Manor Barns, New Road, Barton, Cambridgeshire CB3 7BD (quilting supplies – fabrics)

United States

Come Quilt With Me, 3903 Ave. I, Brooklyn, NY 11210 (718) 377-3652
Keepsake Quilting, Route 25, PO Box 1618, Center Harbor, NH 03226 (603) 253-8731
Nancy's Notions, PO Box 683, Beaver Dam, WI 53916 (800) 833-0690
Quilter's Resource, PO Box 148850, Chicago, IL 60624 (313) 278-5695
Quilts & Other Comforts, 6700 West 44th Ave., Wheatridge, CO 80033 (303) 420-4272
G. Street Fabrics, 11854 Rockville Pike, Rockville, MD 20852 (301) 231-8998
Clotilde, 2 Sew Smart Way B8031, Stevens Point, WI 54481-8031 (800) 772-2891
Fabric Center, 488 Electric Ave., PO Box 8212, Fitchburgh, MA 01420-8212 (508) 343-4402
Mill Creek Fabrics, 295 Fifth Ave., New York, NY 10016 (212) 532-8670

Organizations

In the United Kingdom: National Patchwork Association, PO Box 300, Hethersett, Norwich, Norfolk NR9 3DB
The Quilters' Guild, Unit P66, Dean Clough, Halifax, West Yorkshire HX3 5AX (publish a quarterly full-colour magazine which is sent to members)
(Both previously named organizations will put inquirers in touch with local patchwork/quilting groups.)
The American Museum in Britain, Claverton Manor, Bath, Avon BA2 7BD (permanent exhibition of fine early American quilts)

In the United States: American Quilters' Society, PO Box 3290, Paducah, KY 42002
American International Quilt Association, 7660 Woodway, Suite 550, Houston, TX 77063
National Quilting Association, PO Box 393, Ellicott City, MD 21041-0393
American Quilt Study Group, 660 Mission St., Suite 400, San Francisco, CA 94105